DETAIL IN CONTEMPORARY OFFICE DESIGN

Published in 2014 by
Laurence King Publishing Ltd
361–373 City Road
London
EC1V 1LR
email: enquiries@laurenceking.com
www.laurenceking.com

A catalogue record for this book is
available from the British Library

ISBN: 978 1 78067 340 0

Designed by Olga Reid
Project Editor: Gaynor Sermon
Cover design by Hamish Muir

Printed in China

DETAIL IN CONTEMPORARY OFFICE DESIGN

**DREW PLUNKETT
AND OLGA REID**

LAURENCE KING PUBLISHING

CONTENTS

INTRODUCTION

Working in an office can be a matter of pride, the first evidence of social progression, of a move from physical labour to a more lucrative activity in a comfortable environment. Alternatively, it can suggest lives that are dull and circumscribed. Regardless of general perceptions of office life there are gradations within the spectrum of activities. Processes that require little decision making are ranked low and those that involve creative thinking, whether in fields of financial speculation or design specialism, are rated highly. Organisations, whether staid or progressive, need to provide an environment in which employees can happily and healthily spend half their waking hours. Whether in low ceilinged, ribbon windowed, purpose-built shells or in the resuscitated idiosyncrasies of an abandoned hulk, office workers perhaps have more time to consider the merits of their allotted place than the inhabitants of any other interior.

All offices should convince those who visit them that the organisation they house is reputable, and they should persuade potential employees that they would be happy to share the culture and ethos of their employer. While it is relatively simple to suggest efficiency and probity to outsiders with well appointed reception areas and meeting rooms, the expression of values must be taken beyond front of house to consolidate the loyalty of employees. Enviable working conditions are increasingly seen as an effective seduction and retention tool and organisations may have to find a balance between expenditure on salaries and upgrading the working environment. While a significant pay increase or promotion will always attract good staff, a better working environment that flatters the individual and promotes social interaction will counteract minor dissatisfactions that might otherwise cause employees to move elsewhere. The best offices are not necessarily opulent: for some businesses, some employees and some clients that could be inappropriate. Flamboyance may cause concern about inflated fees, and alienate employees who will expect a proportional rise in pay.

Social history and literature suggests that when office culture first developed in the nineteenth century workers were, if not grateful to their employer, then concerned enough about keeping their job to accept a harsh regime. However, if discipline was hard, the office interiors in which people worked were ornate and well appointed, because that was the habit of the time for all building types other than the most utilitarian. The tradition of well appointed working environments and authoritarian management continued into the twentieth century. There were utopian aspirations, of which one of the most convincing was Frank Lloyd Wright's 'Great Workroom', in fact the administration office for the Johnson Wax company, which can only be described as cathedral-like. A battalion of secretaries, seated in regimented rows beneath a lofty ornately structured ceiling, served the administrators who occupied the mezzanine above them.

Pioneering work on the dedicated modern office building that glorified corporate culture and gave some respect to those who worked in it was a North American phenomenon, concentrated in the financial centres of New York and Chicago. The Empire State Building was the most attention seeking manifestation, but the Chrysler Building and the Rockefeller Center demonstrated the positive effect of lavishly appointed Art Deco interiors that elevated the spirits and the status of those who worked in them.

More modest offices continued to be routinely lined with dull brown wooden panelling. It was not until the post Second World War building boom, initiated by increased prosperity in North America and the necessity of repairing the cities of Europe, that a new aesthetic emerged: shaped by technology and economic expediency, the traditional trappings of success and respectability were replaced with something decidedly more mundane and significantly less likely to engender feelings of enthusiasm for their lot among office workers. The corporate headquarters for Lever Brothers, completed in 1952 on Park Avenue in New York and designed by the emerging, corporate, architectural company of Skidmore, Owings and Merrill, was seen to epitomise the efficiency of standardisation, both in building techniques and office management. Mies Van Der Rohe's building for Seagram, completed across the avenue in 1958, was held to represent the epitome of steel, concrete and glass elegance and, with its front elevation set back from the pavement, it added the 'plaza' to the vocabulary of corporate architecture. Tall entrance lobbies became publicly accessible atriums, following the example of the first one in Kevin Roche's Ford Foundation, completed in 1968.

The stripped-back aesthetic of the Modernist International Style remained the style of choice for corporate office blocks, whether for single or multiple occupations. The stacked floors, sealed permanently shut and augmented by air conditioning, became a universal solution. Demountable partitions of modular plastic laminate covered wall panels, with exposed aluminium frames under a suspended ceiling that concealed servicing ductwork: this became the vocabulary of the office interior. Proximity of desk to ventilating window was no longer a key consideration, and views were reserved for the higher ranking employees whose private offices were planned as multiples of the 1200mm (48 in) module for fenestration and partitioning. The mechanistic rationale of the demountable partition systems seduced architects and designers of the period, not only for the modular determinants that simplified planning decisions but by the promise of flexibility, the potential reconfiguration of the interior to meet changing needs of the business. Adjustment meant, in effect, refit, but the aesthetic sterility of the partitioning systems eliminated the likelihood of change bringing improvement.

Specialist manufacturers, like Steelcase and Knoll, with greater commitment to ergonomic efficiency than employee satisfaction, dominated the market for, and shaped the look of, office furniture. It was only in the hermetic executive zone, typically on top of the tower, that the palette of finishes was expanded. In Europe, however, alternatives were emerging. The 'burolandschaft', or office landscape, movement, which began in Germany in the early 1950s, presented a more worker-centric model. Each employee was given the psychological security of low level screens, normally a modular screen 1200mm (48 in) high, around their work place to which personal memorabilia might be discreetly pinned alongside official memos. Tall plants in big plastic tubs would punctuate the expanse of floor and middle management might share the space.

The principles of 'burolandschaft' were applied in the low ceilinged floors of conventional office blocks. The spaces, screens and furniture continued to look distinctly corporate but the next significant development offered a quite different option. In 1972 Central Beheer, an insurance company's office complex in Apeldoorn in the Netherlands designed by Herman Hertzberger, rejected the omnipresent horizontality and materials palette. It stacked work places around tight, toplit atria. Walls, high and low, were unpainted concrete blocks set into an exposed concrete frame. Workspaces were intimate, enclosed by solid walls but with long views across the internal voids. Workers were encouraged to display personal effects. The justification for the concept continued to stress the capacity to deal with organisational change, but that flexibility was delivered in something that was the antithesis of fragile demountable partitions and acoustic tiled ceilings. Centraal Beheer is now known for its humorous advertising, and it is interesting to speculate whether something already in the corporate mindset led to it commissioning this extraordinary break from office building tradition, or whether the spirit nurtured by the building led to the campaigns.

The example of Centraal Beheer was assimilated, but the manifestations that followed it were restrained and much closer to the general corporate model – unsurprisingly, because its particular aesthetic was hardly universally applicable. Only in a few offices for the creative industries were alternative organisational structures and aesthetics employed. The acceptance of the importance of employee-orientated working environments as generators of productivity and loyalty did however permeate the sector.

Physical evidence of the stratification of management levels and the separation of management and managed staff have been diluted. Flexible working hours and relaxed dress codes recognise the individuality of the employee. Subsidised or free canteens, now more likely to be designated cafes or restaurants, are offered as expressions of concern for employee welfare: the idea of the organisation as family and the social ethos they embody has influenced the aesthetics and layouts of office furniture. Frivolity, sometimes witty sometimes not, is replacing gravitas, sometimes pompous, sometimes not. It might be that the infantilisation of society in general, identified by some social commentators, is invading office culture. It may be appropriate for some activities but the more sober professions do, and presumably will continue to, appropriately, abstain.

Whatever the status or perception of particular office activities, the whole of the sector has been transformed, as fundamentally as every other aspect of daily lives, by digital technologies – not only in the way work is carried out but in the new roles that have been created and old roles that have become defunct. The computer has eliminated the need for many of the lowlier support activities. As the problems of making neat versions of text have been eliminated so typing pools have disappeared, and those who once generated workload for typists now work directly on their own keyboards. Digital communication and information transfer have largely eliminated the need for telephonists and post rooms and, while the paperless office has not become a reality, the sifting and methodical storage of hardcopy has been drastically reduced. Such support staff now fill other roles, moving up to become 'personal assistants' or sideways to perform in call centres.

One fundamental change is that the basic work tool, the computer, is also the basic recreational tool. This has the advantage of diluting the capacity of what is a piece of equipment with extraordinary capabilities to alienate or inhibit those who use it, and this blurs the distinctions between work and leisure. The ageing workforce that struggles to adapt nears extinction.

A culture of the office as a second home, perhaps even superior to the first, is prevailing, and in the offices devoted to the development, application and support of digital innovation, a playground aesthetic has become the norm. The entrepreneurs of digital industries are young, those who have grown up playing digital games and for whom the development of software is a continuation of play. Those who are now leaders were recently innovators and they understand instinctively the free-range ethos of creativity. Never having operated in a culture that persuaded them otherwise, they are committed to the premise that, to flourish, creativity needs to be treated with what to traditionalists would seem to be indulgence. It is an article of their faith that they do not belong to the culture and environment of the traditional office and they express it first in their dress codes and, when they achieve success, in the interiors they commission. Fortunately for the interior designer, those interiors continue to be gratifyingly physical.

A RED OBJECT, SHANGHAI
3GATTI

The brief was to convert a former factory building into offices, with versatile spaces, meeting rooms and a small café. The floor-to-ceiling height of the existing shell prompted the idea of two mezzanines that hugged the existing windows, connected by two bridges. The resulting central void made feasible the creation of the extraordinary free-standing 'red object' and the opportunities for it to be viewed from different angles and from different heights.

While the red object is flamboyant, the planning and realization of the remainder of the accommodation is rational. The layout of office furniture relates sensibly to windows, columns and beams. The new reception desk lines through precisely with a corner of the mezzanine above it. If the floor plans of the meeting rooms are perhaps a little tight the compression is justified because it leaves more space around the object and allows a more emphatic sculpting of its exterior surfaces. Meticulous planning has also squeezed a small kitchen into the object at ground level and, like the door to the meeting room, it is located away from the entrance so that the abstract purity of the object is not diluted by an overtly practical component.

While the object has plasticity it also has the solidity of traditional construction. The inner structural core of brickwork walls and concrete floor eliminates the resonances of lightweight construction and allows the bulbous bulk of the finished outer skin, of plasterboard on timber studwork, to be hoisted above floor level, creating a slot that conceals the light source that washes across the resin floor and, since it also stops short of the ceiling, the object presents itself as a wholly independent entity. All its exterior elements are fine-tuned. The acrylic windowpanes, which sit framelessly in deep slots, make only the most perfunctory references to the rectangle and are equally disdainful of floor levels. Door openings similarly disregard the rectangle.

The reception desk acts as a stylistic bridge between the expressionistic object and the rational mezzanines. Its spray painted MDF skin on its steel frame reads as substantially solid and its white base is both a continuation of the balustrade of the stair and facetted like the object. The raw concrete of the original columns and the new stair relate convincingly to the simplicity of the mezzanines. White paint provides surfaces that reflect the red of the object and the colour not only dramatises its presence in the pristine white context but, traditionally, symbolises joy and luck in China.

RIGHT
The mass of the tower, the shape and location of its windows give no clues to the nature or function of its interior.

Its heavily facetted and hypersmooth red skin contrast with the comparative restraint of the existing columns, the only other vertical elements.

PLAN, GROUND FLOOR, SCALE 1:200

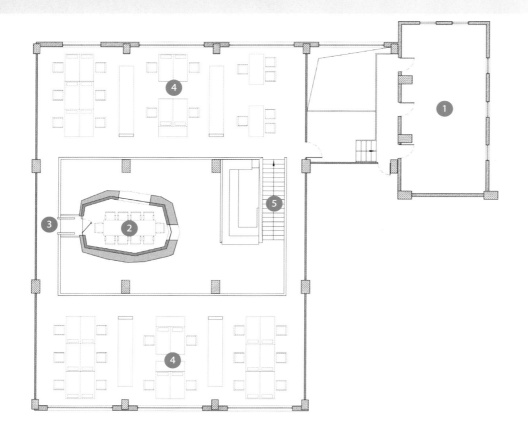

PLAN, FIRST FLOOR, SCALE 1:200

LEFT
Ground Floor Plan
1 Reception desk
2 Meeting room
3 Work area
4 Kitchen (recessed into tower)
5 Storage
6 Stair to mezzanine

BOTTOM
First Floor Plan
1 Void
2 Meeting room
3 Bridge
4 Mezzanine work space
5 Stair to ground floor

OPPOSITE TOP
Section
1 Atrium
2 Meeting room
3 Work area

OPPOSITE MIDDLE LEFT
Although its vertical face helps explain the thickness and modelling of the tower's skin, the door leaf and the windows cut into it conform to its anarchic geometry. The threshold slab, like the tower itself, floats above a shadow gap.

OPPOSITE BOTTOM LEFT
On the upper level users continue to have an intimate relationship with the particularities of the tower's shell.

OPPOSITE BOTTOM RIGHT
The reception desk, second major new element, has some of the tower's panache and acts as a bridge between it and the orthogonal organisation of the rest of the interior.

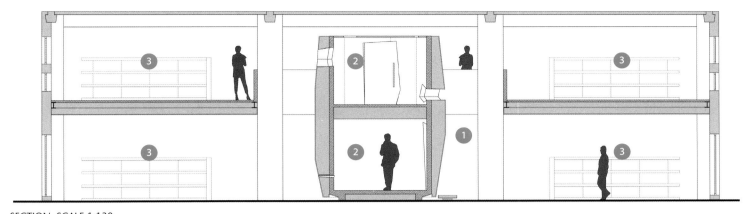

SECTION, SCALE 1:130

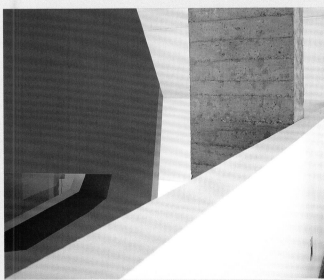

LEFT
Vertical brick walls and a reinforced concrete floor provided the core structure.

BOTTOM LEFT
The brick was rendered and the facets roughly marked out on it in chalk.

BOTTOM RIGHT
Plywood sections provided a solid armature on which the facetted planes were built.

OPPOSITE TOP LEFT
Pre-fabricated sections were used for the more complex sections.

OPPOSITE MIDDLE LEFT
The plywood was covered with plasterboard and joints and screw head recesses filled for final refinement of the form before painting.

OPPOSITE BOTTOM LEFT
A similar construction sequence was followed for the reception desk.

OPPOSITE TOP RIGHT
A white undercoat was applied to seal surfaces before the final coats of red.

OPPOSITE BOTTOM RIGHT
Light, reflected off the red surfaces, tints the white walls and floor.

RED TOWN, SHANGHAI
TARANTA CREATIONS

Ergonomics, unimaginatively applied, make insipid interiors but creative ambition, prompted by the vagaries of an awkward site, finds a way to transcend the prosaic. Red Town, designed within a former metal works for and by its occupants, was seized upon as an opportunity to explore the creative process and demonstrate practical abilities.

The occupants wanted an adaptable and informal work place and found it in their pragmatic response to problems presented by existing roof trusses. If they deployed a conventional floor to ceiling height on the ground floor the bottom member of the truss would sit about 800mm (31½ in) above the upper floor and users would be obliged to clamber over it, but the insertion of the upper floor just above the bottom member of the truss meant that only the more accommodating angled struts needed negotiation and the 2200mm (87 in) floor-to-ceiling height gave adequate headroom. The potential for occupying the zone between lower ceiling and upper floor evolved into recessed workstations, each for two designers who would tuck their knees under the floor plane, which doubled as their work surface. This removed the visual interference of chairs, desks and storage so that the floor level reads as something nearer to an unbroken plane. A bench built into a side wall and cushions scattered across the floor become places for the more informal, but fundamentally crucial aspects, of the design process.

While this interpretation of the working environment would be enough to establish the interior's identity it is even more emphatically defined by the less pragmatic expression of the stair, which wholly dominates the entrance level. Described as a 'water drop' it appears to hang from the ceiling, like a drip on the point of falling. Its skin of thin plywood panels laid over timber framing makes complex three-dimensional curves that, with joints filled and sanded for a glossy finish of silver paint, melds seamlessly into the ceiling. Its curves are reflected in a bulbous high green table, designated for informal meetings, and the serpentine edge of the raised floor along the window wall on which sit the workstations. A narrow stairway cut through this seeming solid curves slightly in response to the bulbous form that contains it. Each tread is cantilevered from a central spine and lit beneath so that it appears to float within the hollowed out core.

RIGHT
The red slot of the stair cuts through the 'waterdrop'. The red is reminiscent of the Chinese flag and perhaps also implies raw incisions cut into the new solids.

OPPOSITE
The ground floor is organised around and visually dominated by the globular form of the stair enclosure. The green communal table shares its bulbous profile.

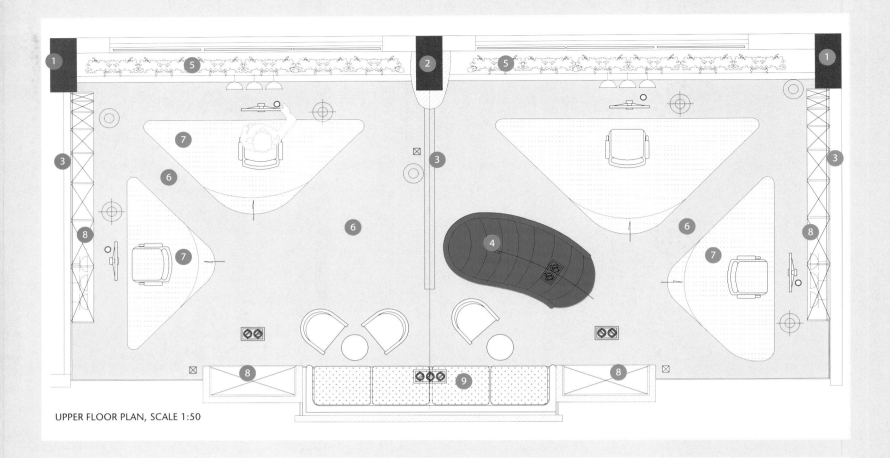

UPPER FLOOR PLAN, SCALE 1:50

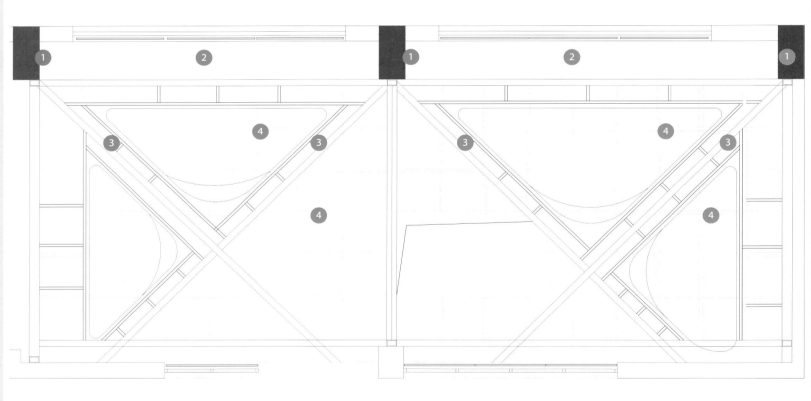

PLAN, NEW STRUCTURE, SCALE 1:50

OPPOSITE TOP

Upper Floor Plan
1 Existing structural column
2 Re-clad existing structural column
3 Structural roof joist
4 Stair to lower level
5 Void
6 New floor level
7 Desk recess
8 Storage
9 Seating

OPPOSITE BOTTOM

Plan: New Structure
1 Existing structural column
2 Void
3 New structural beams
4 New timber floor structure

TOP

The existing roof truss, behind the red balustrades of the stair, determines the new floor level. Recessed work places, each for two people with inner surfaces red to match the stair, use the new floor as a work surface.

RIGHT

A curved step eases entry to the work station, knee spaces and storage slots are cut into the void below floor level. The roof truss bisects a built-in bench and shelving.

ABOVE
Thin plywood panels were fixed to a timber frame and plastered to give the smooth profile of the 'waterdrop'.

LEFT
Storage on the end wall is organised to suit the geometry of the roof truss. Cushions accommodate squatted discussions.

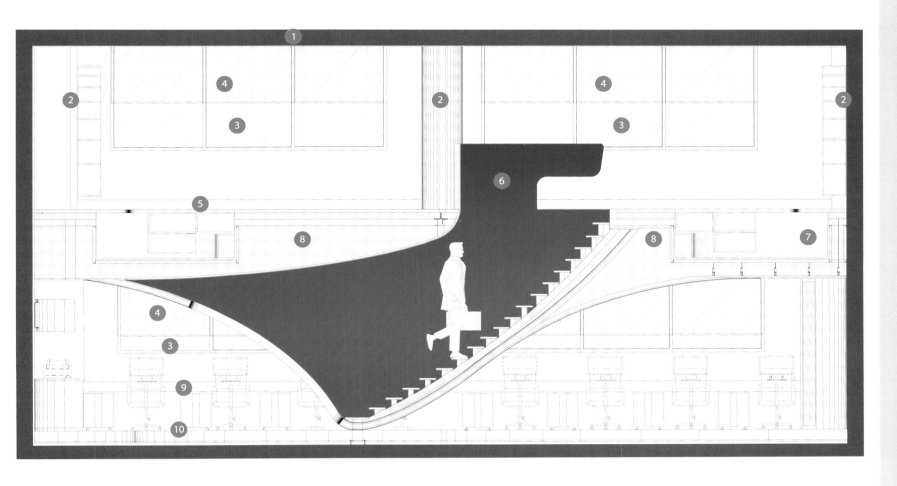

SECTION, SCALE 1:50

ABOVE

1 Existing roof structure
2 Re-clad structural column
3 Window beyond void
4 Blind
5 Upstand to void
6 Stair balustrade
7 Recessed work station
8 Plywood clad stair structure
9 Work bench
10 Raised and curved floor level

RIGHT

As it rises the stair bends slightly, to acknowledge the organic bulges of its enclosure.

IMD,
ROTTERDAM
ECTOR HOOGSTAD ARCHITECTS

The monumentality and materiality of derelict industrial sheds can evoke nostalgia and excite imaginations, even if the exterior skin is unprepossessing. The clients who chose to reclaim this former steel plant are leading design engineers and thought that the building's history made it an appropriate base for their business. After initial investigations with their architects, with whom they had already completed a number of successful projects, they decided that structural refurbishment and environmental upgrading of the existing shell were technically and financially unrealistic but, as is often the case, the first proposal gave way to an unanticipated and quirkier outcome after a more tangential reconsideration of the first idea.

In the revision, work areas are housed on two levels, behind skins of corrugated, translucent plastic sheets, and are independent of the original structure but set against blank end walls of the existing building. These have views back into the original volume, in which pavilions, serving as conference rooms, are connected by a network of stairs and footbridges that encourage exploration and casual interaction. The reduced volumes of the new structures, with their energy efficient skins are more effectively air-conditioned. The hall itself remains less environmentally efficient but serves adequately for discussions, lectures, exhibitions and as a staff café. Large new windows open up views to the nearby River Maas and combine with existing rooflights to flood the interior with natural light so that it assumes some of qualities of an outdoor area, an illusion fostered by the café's picnic benches and floor of digitally reproduced vegetation.

The existing steel structure, the concrete floor and the brick skin have been cleaned and the limited palette of new materials – glass and plastic sheets, rough timber for stairs – sits comfortably and confidently within that extant industrial aesthetic. The clear glass and translucent plastic reveal, with different intensities, the bright yellow paint used throughout the newly constructed interiors and, although the plastic half reveals the structural framing that supports it, its reflectivity and the intensity of the yellow paint results in simpler, more assertive, albeit more fragile, forms that dominate the comparative confusion of the much more substantial structural elements and the matt surfaces of the original building.

TOP
New windows pierce the brick skin of the existing steel works.

MIDDLE
The elements of the new insertions, clear glass, transparent plastic sheet, yellow paint and rough timber, assert their presence at the point of entry.

BOTTOM
The steel framing of the translucent walls has the same robust, engineered directness as the existing structural roof elements.

RIGHT
The natural illumination of the translucent cladding gives it an affinity with the existing rooflights.

BOTTOM
Long section

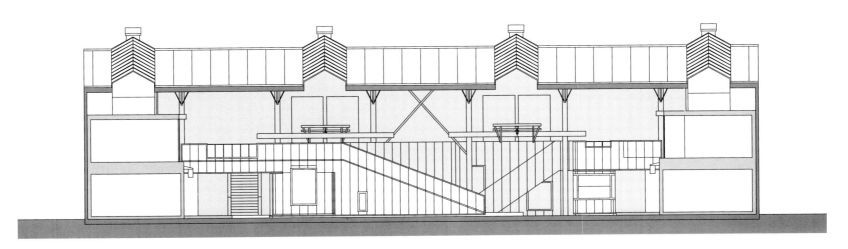

SECTION, SCALE 1:200

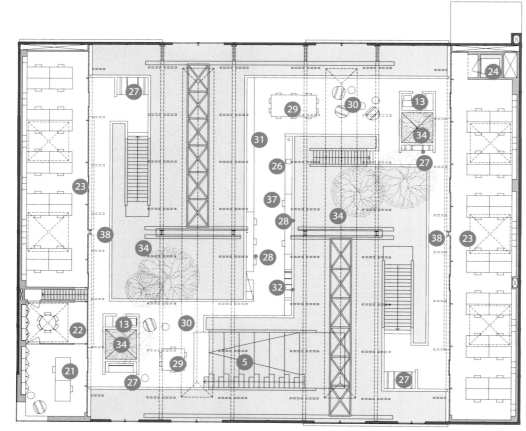

FIRST FLOOR PLAN, SCALE 1:300

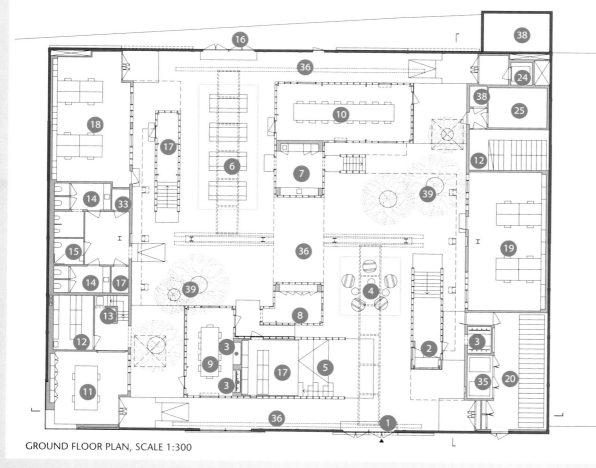

GROUND FLOOR PLAN, SCALE 1:300

OPPOSITE TOP LEFT
The light flex and bulb holders share the yellow that is the only applied colour in the interior. The rough raw timber of the stair matches the hues and textures of existing surfaces.

OPPOSITE TOP RIGHT
The painted floors and ceilings beneath the areas of upper floor clearly contrast with the brutality of the existing shell.

OPPOSITE BOTTOM LEFT
The precise translucent wall, which gives views of spectral figures moving beyond it, also provides a commonality between raw timber flooring and benching 'outside' and the smooth surfaces 'inside'.

OPPOSITE BOTTOM RIGHT
Picnic tables define an eating and meeting place. The plastic floor covering, with its digitally printed grass and flowers, helps imply that the space outside the translucent walls is a kind of exterior.

STUDIO IN THE WOODS, MADRID
SELGAS CANO ARCHITECTS

Interiors, and not just those for offices, are normally about making good the shortcomings of an existing shell, whether in response to a change of use or to improve users' experience. It might be argued that this project for the designers' own studio is more about the exterior than the interior, but the relationship of the two, and their connection to their context, is so interlinked that it offers an example of how thinking about the experience of being inside shapes decisions about the exterior and demonstrates how a shared detailing language evolves.

The creation of the building was prompted by the designers' desire to 'work under the trees'. They half buried the single storey so that the external ground level broadly coincided with internal eye levels, sitting or standing. The designers wanted maximum transparency but realised that, even amongst trees, clear glazing had to be confined to the north side, to reduce heat gain and to prevent sunlight shining directly on work surfaces. So the north elevation and half the roof is fabricated from continuous sheets of 20mm (¾ in) clear acrylic sheet, with a curved transition from vertical to horizontal and milled at the edges to enable silicon sealant to be injected into joints. The southern section of roof and wall, with the same curved profile, is a 110mm (4¾ in) sandwich of translucent insulation between sheets of natural coloured fibreglass and polyester, which allows some light penetration. Its internal face bears shadowy traces of the steel frame and is dappled by the sunlight that penetrates the trees above it. The unique nature of the construction demanded unique materials and components. One, a curved roof section, was produced in Denmark exclusively for the German railway and it was necessary to wait for them to place an order before the production line could viably restart.

The imprint of the shuttering boards' wood grain marks the surface of internal concrete retaining walls and, when painted green relates very directly to surrounding trees. Wooden floorboards are finished with an epoxy-based paint and the line of colour change, between work places and the circulation zone, corresponds exactly to the junction of translucent and transparent roofs. The thin bent tubular brackets and the clear acrylic shelves they support are miniaturised variations of the glazing components.

Apart from its semi-subterranean element the project uses few, if any, traditional building materials and calls on few, if any, traditional building skills. Innovative detailing became contagious and led to the ingeniously complex door between studio and office and the ventilation system operated by pulleys and counterweights.

TOP
The semi-subterranean installation, transparency and reflectivity reduce the building's presence.

BOTTOM
For ventilation the end panel may be hoisted open by a pulley and held in place by counterbalancing weights.

OPPOSITE
Plan
1 Exterior steps
2 Entrance
3 Dividing wall and door

4 Large office
5 Small office
6 Steps to lower level
7 Lavatory
8 Store

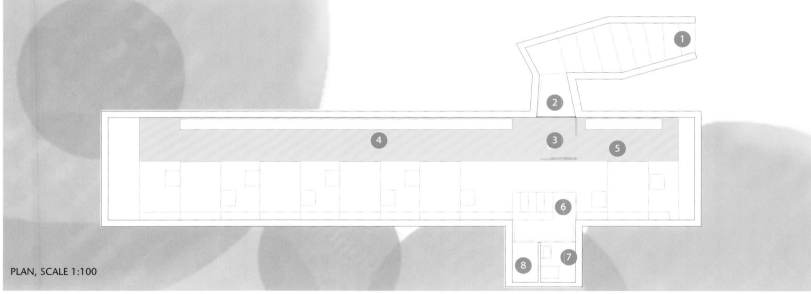

PLAN, SCALE 1:100

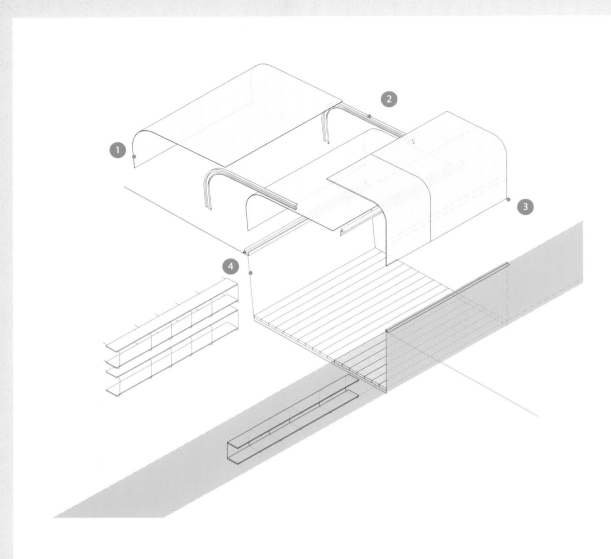

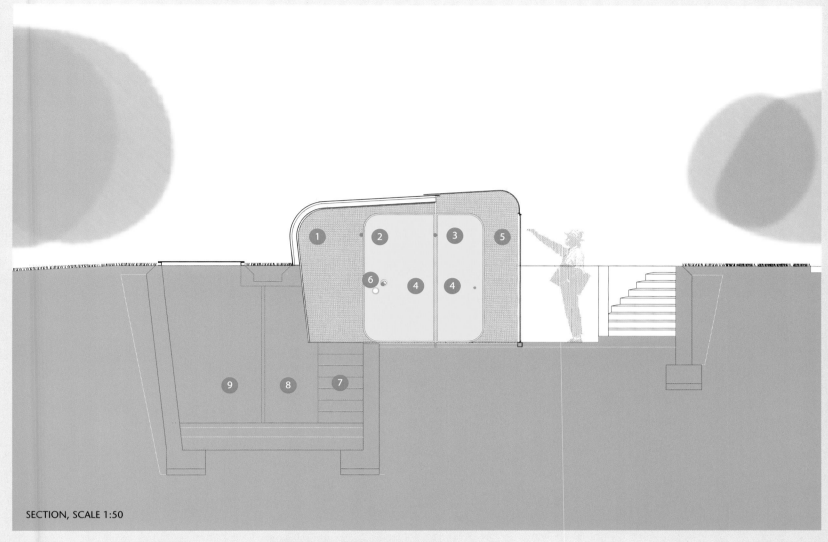

SECTION, SCALE 1:50

LEFT

White tables are cantilevered from the white wall. Bent metal 'D' brackets support clear acrylic shelving. The yellow tubular finned radiator pipes bridge the junction of yellow floor and green wall.

BOTTOM LEFT

Typical Cross Section
1 Translucent roof/wall sheet
2 Steel structural rib
3 Transparent roof/wall sheet
4 Concrete retaining wall
5 Clear acrylic shelves on tubular brackets
6 Cantilevered work table
7 Radiator
8 Mechanism for side wall ventilation

OPPOSITE TOP LEFT

The heavy textures of the concrete retaining wall, cast in-situ, make a visual connection between the smooth acrylic skin and the trees beyond it.

OPPOSITE TOP RIGHT

Shelf Detail
1 Clear acrylic shelf
2 Painted tubular bracket
3 Finned radiator
4 Concrete retaining wall
5 Floor finish
6 Concrete subfloor

OPPOSITE BOTTOM

The smaller office area beyond the entrance may be opened up to the studio. When closed the leaves of the orange door float visually in the fixed, clear acrylic-edge panels. The door sections open asymmetrically along the line of the floor and roof junctions and the smaller half performs as a conventional door when the separation is in place.

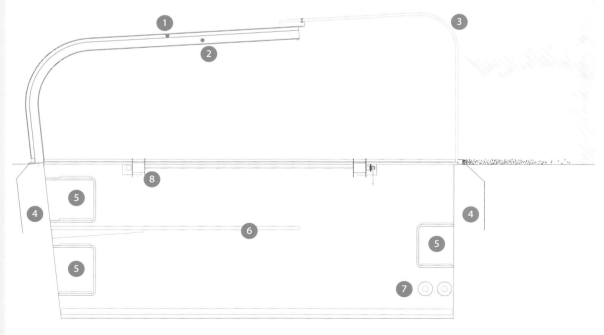

SECTION, SCALE 1:35

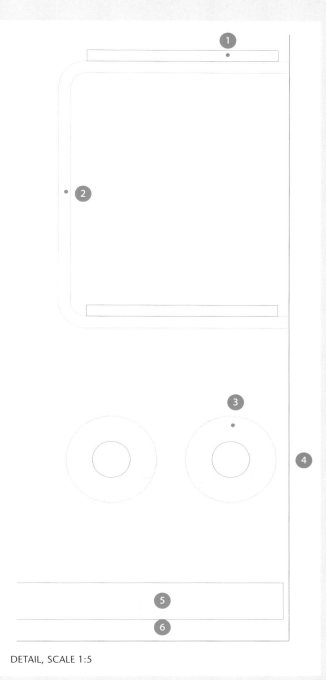

DETAIL, SCALE 1:5

KKCG, PRAGUE
VRTIŠKA + ŽÁK WITH ATELIER RAW

Increasingly hard-nosed businesses are keen to subscribe to ecological principles and to have that commitment expressed in the buildings they inhabit. KKCG is a financial and investment company and, while having other interests, it specialises in areas relating to the extraction of oil and gas and asserts its concern that its activities should be carried out responsibly.

Small and overtly ecological businesses can wholly embrace the approved environmental palette of materials and construction techniques but that is less applicable for a company occupying six floors of a modern office block and with diverse activities that are not exclusively ecological. For KKCG the designers introduced natural elements as set pieces among what is otherwise a familiar office landscape. The building has, at its core, a twenty-one metre high atrium, approached through a low ceilinged lobby, and this they lined with white aluminium ribs that writhe and twist as they rise to the rooflight, mimicking the unpredictable irregularity of a natural form. Powerful and elegant as this metallic skin may be it is upstaged by the phenomenon of a vertical garden of living plants, watered and fed by a computer controlled irrigation system, that wraps around the walls of the stair well and rises the height of the atrium. Other 'living walls' are distributed throughout the building to define and embellish informal meeting areas and plant life is deployed more whimsically inside the stairwell where clusters of sedums make up the two metre high numbers that mark each floor level.

Other natural materials are few but wide oak flooring boards are used to clad the exterior walls and interior surfaces of the fifth floor meeting rooms which are detailed to look free-standing. Their raised floor levels allow a thick oak strip to frame the window that wholly occupies one wall of the room on its four edges and, at an opposite end of the technological spectrum, the window's composite glass can change from transparent to opaque when an electric current charges its conductive core. There are no plants in the hard harsh environment of the ground floor gymnasium but the commitment to green hues and values is made plain by the bright studded rubber flooring and the changing rooms' oak boarded skin, which counterpoint the raw concrete of walls and ceiling. In the subterranean parking garage every wall, floor, ceiling and service duct is painted apple green, except at the junctions of walls and columns with the ceiling where a white band allows the green to transmute into blades of painted grass.

GROUND FLOOR PLAN, SCALE 1:1000

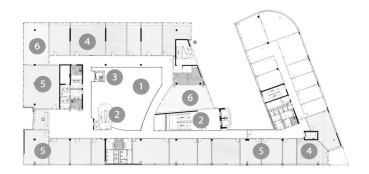

TYPICAL OFFICE FLOOR PLAN, SCALE 1:1000

LEVEL FIVE PLAN, SCALE 1:1000

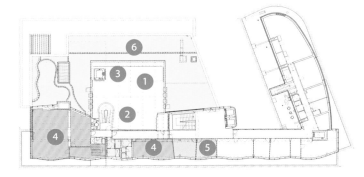

LEVEL SIX PLAN, SCALE 1:000

OPPOSITE TOP

The solid block of the reception desks contrasts with the skeletal ribs of the atrium and restaurant. Proprietary light fittings complement its simplicity.

ABOVE

At the entrance the reception desk sits back to maximise the impact of the low space between white floor and white ceiling transmuting into the atrium. A section of the hard white ribs hangs against the 'living wall'.

OPPOSITE MIDDLE

Ground Floor Plan
1 Covered arrival court
2 Entrance
3 Reception
4 Lobby/atrium
5 Stair
6 Lift
7 Restaurant

OPPOSITE BOTTOM

Plan: Typical Office Floor
1 Atrium void
2 Stair

3 Lift
4 Manager's office
5 Standard office
6 Meeting room

MIDDLE

Level Five Plan
1 Atrium void
2 Stair
3 Lift
4 Meeting room
5 'Living wall'
6 Principal's office
7 Manager's office
8 Standard office
9 Relaxation room
10 Lower roof terrace

BOTTOM

Level Six Plan
1 Atrium void
2 Stair
3 Lift
4 Principal's office
5 Standard office
6 Upper roof terrace

LEFT
Amid the obsessive whiteness of lacquered aluminium ribs, echoed in the pleated lines of white chairs and lampshades, a 'living wall' of vegetation wraps around the stair tower.

BOTTOM LEFT
The planted stair tower climbs twenty-one metres to the rooflight. Mirror balls hanging in the atrium suggest enormous raindrops.

OPPOSITE TOP
Ribs climbing through the void create mutating three-dimensional patterns.

OPPOSITE BOTTOM LEFT
'Living graphics' mark out floor levels.

OPPOSITE BOTTOM RIGHT
In widened corridor areas, bulbously organic chairs, their colours matching the illuminated wall panels, sit on deep-piled rugs, around a tree trunk table, beside a suspended plastic curtain that shares the organic intricacies of the 'living wall'.

OPPOSITE TOP LEFT
Meeting rooms are clad in solid timber boards on a wooden frame.

OPPOSITE TOP RIGHT
Proprietary glass, which becomes translucent or opaque when an electrical charge is passed through it, brings degrees of visual privacy to meeting rooms. A planted wall defines an informal meeting place off the corridor circling the atrium.

OPPOSITE BOTTOM
The wooden cladding continues on the interior.

TOP LEFT
The gymnasium is a tougher space although the timber clad changing rooms sustain an organic presence amongst the exposed mechanical services, harsh lights and acidic green rubber floor.

TOP RIGHT
The interior of the changing rooms continues the robust colour palette.

BOTTOM LEFT
The black and yellow hazard stripes work well with the apple green which peters out in a suggestion of grass.

BOTTOM RIGHT
The subterranean parking garage is invigorated by the bright green paint and giant graphics in the international lingua franca.

BUSINESS STREAM, EDINBURGH
GRAVEN IMAGES

Business Stream is a subsidiary of a major water providing company, but a significant requirement in their brief was that their new reception, the shared and private office areas, the meeting rooms and cafe should establish a distinctive identity for them. The declaration of independence begins as visitors arrive, with a vigorous and attention seeking reconsideration of the conventional reception desk. Square edged blocks of storage furniture and flat working surfaces are hidden behind a flamboyantly sculpted MDF carapace, spray painted to read as a monolithic abstraction. The legal obligation to lower an area of desk to accommodate wheel chair users prompted, and becomes a pretext for, decisions about the massing of the whole. The space beneath the lowered level, which is free of storage units, is left open to allow those in wheel chair to tuck their legs between its heavily facetted supports.

On an adjacent white wall white three-dimensional letters present the first explicit expression of company values and this message wall extends into a 'touchdown internet' area that is a buffer between reception and the office proper. That threshold is formally marked by a battery of fins, clearly separated from floor and ceiling by steel rods that suggest they might pivot and close. A different interpretation of fins appears in the café. A solid line of banquettes, which with the lower blocks that separate them, are a castellated wall that marks the boundary separating the café from the circulation route that skirts the window to the central courtyard. Thin fins that mimic the curtain wall fenestration to the courtyard rise from the top of the banquette backrest and turn through ninety degrees to become a canopy that further defines the zone. A wall of the café is decorated with circular photographs of employees, crudely cropped to imply that inclusivity is spontaneous and without undue ceremony. The colours of the circles occupying the remainder of the wall are those of the company logo and the bigger circles suggest that other faces will be added to the wall as the company prospers.

Spheres, inspired by the graded circles and colours of the logo hang above the ranks of workstations declaring key words from the mission statement. Logo-hued letters also spell out words and phrases on appropriate walls. Their directness is counterbalanced by more abstracted images that hint at geographical context.

ABOVE
The standard massing of a reception desk, with a lower level for wheelchair users and a higher front shielding the work surface, is facetted and twisted close to the point of abstraction. The indented arches and circles in the wall and door behind share the geometry of the light fittings.

RIGHT
Reception desk.

knowledge
dependable res

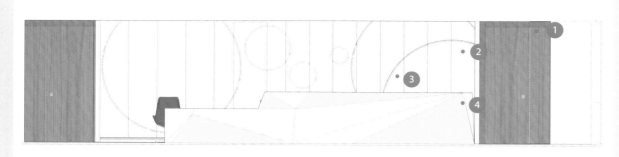

FRONT ELEVATION, SCALE 1:75

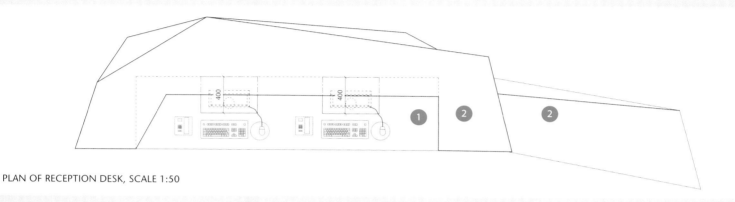

PLAN OF RECEPTION DESK, SCALE 1:50

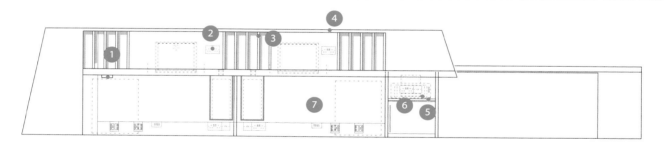

REAR ELEVATION, SCALE 1:50

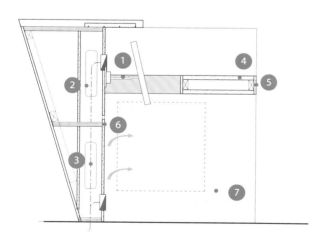

SECTION, SCALE 1:20

RIGHT
Circles of casually cropped snapshots of workers decorate one wall of the café. Thin fins rise from the backrest of the banquette and bend back across the ceiling.

BOTTOM LEFT & RIGHT
Motivational adjectives adorn walls and float above shared work spaces.

effortless
dependable
responsive
knowledgeable
progressive

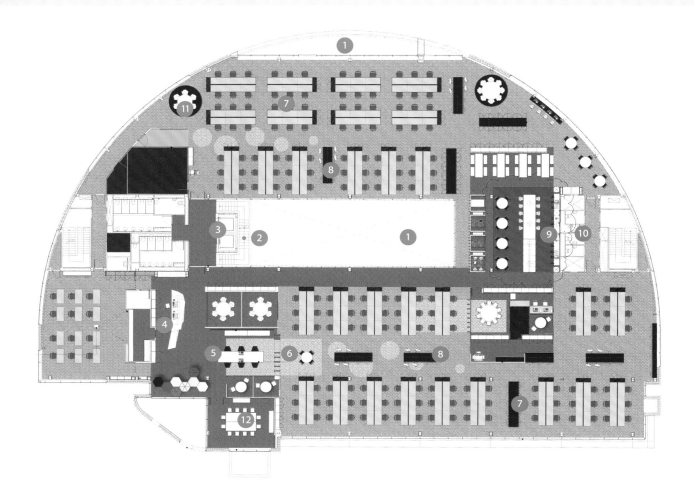

PLAN, SCALE 1:250

ABOVE

Plan

1 Void
2 Internal stair
3 Lift
4 Reception
5 Touchdown internet
6 Fin screen
7 Shared office
8 Storage cabinet
9 Banquette
10 Café
11 Team meeting table
12 Board room

BOTTOM LEFT

A chunky unbroken run of banquettes separates the café area from the circulation area that skirts the central void housing the internal stair and lift tower.

BOTTOM RIGHT

A screen of fins partially isolates a touchdown internet area from the open plan office for meetings and presentations.

TOP LEFT

Section at Edge Panel

1 Plasterboard bulkhead on softwood framing with taped, filled and painted joints

2 12mm (½ in) high gloss lacquered MDF on softwood framing with 10mm (⅜ in) shadow gap to bulkhead

3 High gloss lacquered MDF skirting with 10mm (⅜ in) shadow gap to vertical face

Section Through Bulkhead Between Fins

1 Plasterboard bulkhead on softwood framing with taped, filled and painted joints

2 10mm (⅜ in) shadow gap to horizontal head element

3 Brushed stainless steel support

4 Fins with 12mm (½ in) high gloss lacquered MDF on softwood framing

TOP RIGHT

Brushed stainless steel supports free the lacquered fins visually from floor and ceiling.

MIDDLE

Elevation: Fins

1 Painted plasterboard bulkhead with taped and filled joints on softwood framing

2 High gloss lacquered MDF top and side panels

3 High Gloss lacquered 12mm (½ in) MDF fin cladding

4 Brushed stainless steel support

BOTTOM

Plan: Fins

1 Line of plasterboard bulkhead above

2 High Gloss lacquered 12mm (½ in) MDF fin cladding

3 Softwood framing

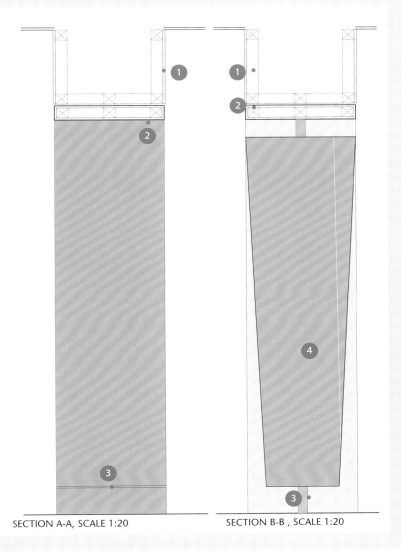

SECTION A-A, SCALE 1:20   SECTION B-B , SCALE 1:20

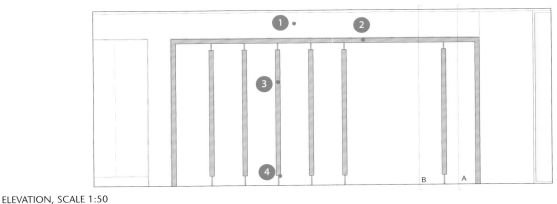

ELEVATION, SCALE 1:50

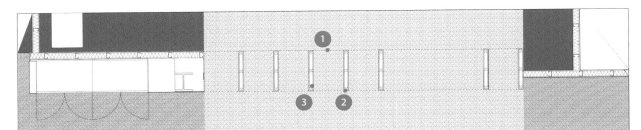

PLAN, SCALE 1:50

JVM,
HAMBURG
STEPHEN WILLIAMS ASSOCIATES

Occasionally the job of giving personality to a company's interior is made easier when a familiar visual identity can be convincingly reinterpreted in the materials and technologies of building. In this project the client, a leading German based advertising agency, was expanding into the two floors they did not already occupy in a former nineteenth century factory building. The accounts department would relocate to the first floor and senior management, their support and the staff café to the fourth. The designers enthusiastically seized upon the agency's logo, an elegantly simplified but heroically poised image of a Trojan Horse, as the inspiration for defining set pieces on each floor.

For the accounts department a long linear piece of what the designers call 'furniture sculpture', incorporating a number of mundane components like copying and printing machines, practical elements like meeting places and whimsical details like dog kennels, occupies a wide central corridor. The diagrammatic simplicity of the logo influences the chunky angled massing of individual sections within the whole. The clearly expressed cladding boards obviously refer to the construction of the horse and the rounded edges to short flights of steps suggest its wooden wheels. The motif is reinterpreted again on the fourth floor in the staff café where the body and neck of the horse are deconstructed and adjusted to become the cross section of a table and banquette seating that is extruded to make a long booth, with the head serving as a high shelf. The floor, walls and ceiling of the area are clad in dark stained timber to suggest the horse's hollow core.

The principal space on the fourth floor is shared by senior management who sit around a single enormous table in the middle of a large but otherwise sparsely furnished room, an arrangement that responded to the agency's unique culture. When necessary, individuals may find privacy in one of two small 'cabins' on the external wall. The room is separated from the corridor by a steel and glass screen that comfortably matches the inflated scale of the table and these monumental elements, along with the status of those who use the room, have caused it to be quickly dubbed the 'elephant house'. Management assistants are paired in offices across the corridor. These and other offices are finished with a collage of colours, soft and textured materials unlike those normally associated with partitioning systems.

TOP
The agency's logo covers one gable of the former factory building.

BOTTOM
The logo shapes the cross section of bench and seating in the staff cafe.

OPPOSITE TOP
The graphic style of the logo also influences the configuration of the continuous element that forms a spine on the accountants' floor.

OPPOSITE BOTTOM
Plan
1 Lift
2 Stairs
3 Entrance area
4 Waiting/meeting room
5 Shared management room

6 Shared private management room
7 Management support
8 Kitchen
9 Communal area
10 Office
12 Gymnasium

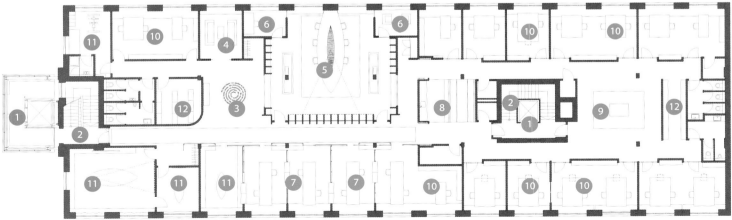

PLAN, SCALE 1:300

TOP & BOTTOM
Chunky timber detailing characterising places to work and relax are set along the spine.

TOP

Text is inlaid into the floor of the entrance area of the management floor.

BOTTOM

A parade of heavy fins frames the glazed wall to the communal accommodation for the agency management.

WER IST WO?

ABOVE
The enormous table, shared by the management team, sits heavily in the centre of the room. It and its ancillary elements share a scale and construction that justifies the room's 'Elephant House' epithet.

LEFT
Management support staff are accommodated in double rooms. Timber inserts in the partitioning system and a loosely folded fabric document storage unit create an appropriately relaxed environment.

TOP LEFT & RIGHT
Vertical sliding hatches that make
strategic connections between adjoining
rooms add to the project's idiosyncratic
informality.

RIGHT
Shelves and white storage bins, one for
each member of the management team,
are serviced by support staff.

LBi,
LONDON
BRINKWORTH

In a former brewing hall, located in an area of East London that has become alternatively fashionable and a hub for creative industries, LBi, Europe's biggest digital agency, wanted to establish an office that would accommodate all of their five hundred staff, who had been scattered in a number of sites across the city. They wanted an interior that would declare their creativity and energy.

The designers took advantage of the sprawling floor area of the original shell, in excess of five thousand square metres area with ten metre high spaces to cut voids and hang mezzanines. They began by upgrading the existing façades, replacing sections of the front with full-height translucent glass channels and glazing the entire rear elevation to open up views over the east of the city. The additional glazing bathes the new three storey atrium in natural light and the floor slab was cut back to allow it to infiltrate the basement. A web of new I-section steel beams support the bridge that forms the entrance to the building. A splayed black reception desk occupies the centre of the bridge and visitors skirt the edges of the void to reach the waiting area on its other side. Below them they see the coloured arcs that mark out the grey floor of the sports hall which, with an auditorium for presentations and a canteen, occupies the basement

The geometric precision of the desk and the beams and the upholstered luxury of the sofas are directly confronted by evidence of the old, exposed metal fixings and exposed brickwork, tucked under one of the new mezzanines, which are supported on suspension cables that relieve the otherwise impossible burden on existing columns. New mezzanines have also been created and existing ones extended on the upper levels. The resulting voids again allow light to infiltrate greater areas of the interior and again it was feasible to suspend the new elements from the existing structure, eliminating the need for supporting columns that would have compromised the flexibility inherent in the rolling expanses of floor.

Redundant utilitarian elements from the old have been retained and restored. Strong paint colours and raw metals complement these remnants and the most significant example of this interaction is the screen of expanded metal, topped with a 'cornice' of a suspended perforated metal service gantry and lit to cast intricate shadows, that lines the side of an existing ramp and partly conceals an excessive clutter of redundant openings and pipework.

TOP
The existing façade, upgraded with Reglit glazing channels, allows natural light to penetrate the interior more effectively.

RIGHT
The grid of structural beams sits over the basement canteen. The metal mesh screen sets up a single flat plane but, when well lit, does not mask the elements behind it.

TOP

The black MDF reception desk, with a back lit panel towards the entrance door, sits on the bridge that spans the newly opened void to the basement floor. The higher floor level of the bridge continues to the seating area at the original floor level.

RIGHT

Entrance Bridge Details
1 New steel beams
2 New stub supports off existing steel beam
3 Existing steel beams
4 Rolled steel angles at 750mm (30 in) centres welded to plate
5 8mm (⅜ in) plate
6 80mm (3 in) concrete infill
7 Mesh reinforcement to concrete infill

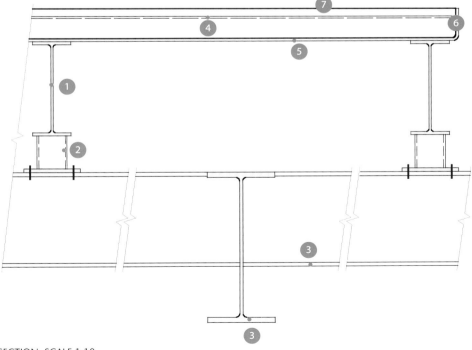

SECTION, SCALE 1:10

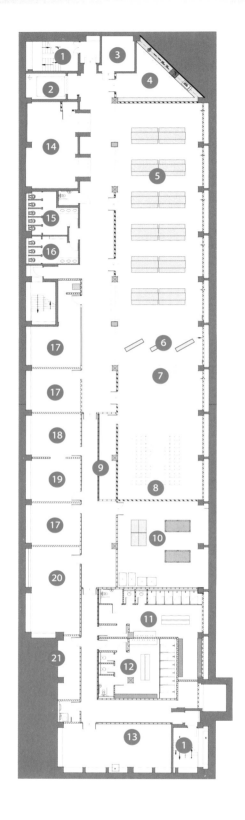

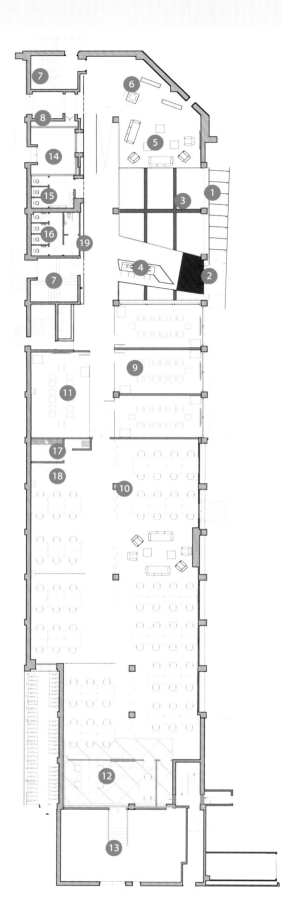

FAR LEFT
Basement Plan
1 Stair
2 Lift
3 Meter room
4 Food preparation and server
5 Canteen
6 Display light boxes
7 Roller shutter door
8 Auditorium
9 Store
10 Games
11 Men's changing
12 Women's changing
13 Boiler room and plant
14 Library
15 Women's lavatory
16 Men's lavatory
17 Breakout room
18 Testing room
19 Observational testing room
20 IT build room
21 Filing room

LEFT
Ground Floor Plan
1 Ramp
2 Entrance
3 Void
4 Reception desk
5 Reception waiting
6 Light boxes
7 Stair
8 Lift
9 Team rooms
10 Workstations
11 Meeting room
12 Dispatch room
13 Plant
14 Electrical substation
15 Men's lavatory
16 Women's and disabled lavatory
17 Kitchen
18 Print station
19 Mesh screen

BASEMENT PLAN, SCALE 1:300

GROUND FLOOR PLAN, SCALE 1:300

TOP LEFT

Detail at Entrance

1 150x150mm (6x6 in) steel beam and fixings painted black satin

2 Boxing conceals plate and structural glass fin bracket

3 Existing column

4 Reglit sill section

5 2mm (⅛ in) folded coloured aluminium sheet flashing

6 flexible weatherproofing

7 2mm (⅛ in) folded aluminium sheet flashing sealed with silicone joint

8 400x10mm (15¾x⅜ in) mild steel plate welded to underside of 150x150mm (6x6 in) beam

9 Overdoor closer concealed by aluminium cladding

10 24mm (⅞ in) double glazed door

11 Door frame surround

12 Letterbox

13 Floor finish

14 Screed infill to steel structure

15 Door closer set in screed

TOP RIGHT

The new mezzanine hangs from the existing roof structure.

BOTTOM LEFT

The mesh screen rises through the ground and first floors. When viewed more obliquely in poorer light it masks the elements behind more significantly. A ramp connects the two first floor levels.

BOTTOM RIGHT

Canteen furniture is simple and robust, in response to the original industrial shell. Markings for games decorate the floor.

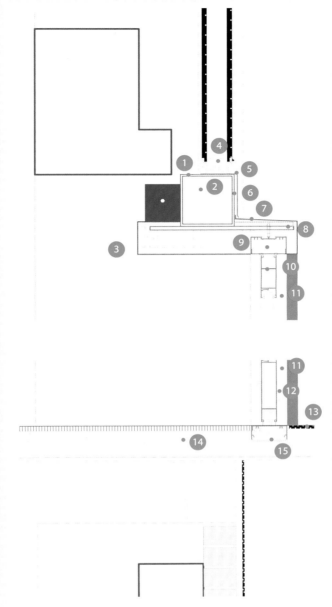

DETAIL, SCALE 1:10

MULBERRY, LONDON
UNIVERSAL DESIGN STUDIO

Clients hope, and ask, that the interior of their office will reflect the nature and values of their business and, normally, this aspiration is met with a broadly generic solution appropriate to the sector in which they operate. However, when clients are producers and retailers of luxury goods, for whom the interior is a crucial component in the definition of their brand ethos, then they are likely to want their offices to embody that same ethos, to offer a stylistic statement to prompt and direct their staff.

Mulberry has built its reputation on finely crafted leather work and a contemporary interpretation of traditional English style. For their new offices they appointed Universal Design Studio, who had also been responsible for their first flagship store in London in which they made references to the English landscape and crafts, with a dry stone wall and skeletal, room-sized oak display structures. These they dubbed 'follies' (a folly traditionally being a visually extravagant building intended primarily for decorative purposes). The idea of the folly wall was transposed to the new offices where it sits, taller and leaner, in a void, rising from basement level to the top of the first floor within a new glazed enclosure that looks on to an upgraded courtyard. The enclosed basement area, known as 'the town square', provides flexible places for meetings, working and lunching: visible from reception, it gives visitors an informal insight into the character of the company.

Visitors enter the office through a stone arch, which is high but does not immediately reveal the top of the 'folly wall' in which the letters of 'Mulberry', in different fonts and materials, are placed. The white boards that form the back of the wall serve the same function as the shop's stone wall and conceal services. The other link to the store is the brass used for some of the letters, the door frames and display furniture. Leather upholstered furniture, a reference to the brand's signature material, is scattered across the entrance space and throughout the building, particularly in the area in front of the stairs and lifts on each floor. Leather sofas, wooden stools and brass light fittings appear throughout the studios where they punctuate the rows of work tables and offer places for informal discussion. In the courtyard a multitude of garden gnomes, milling around a dilapidated garden shed represent a tongue-in-cheek view of 'Englishness'. Mulberry is responsible for such installations and changes them in response to their seasonal merchandising strategies.

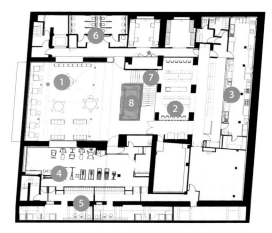

BASEMENT PLAN, SCALE 1:300

TOP
The archway entrance offers a partial view of the toplit 'folly' wall.

RIGHT
Basement Level Plan
1 Line of void above

2 Restaurant
3 Kitchen
4 Gymnasium
5 Changing rooms
6 Lavatories
7 Stair
8 Lift

TOP RIGHT

The view back to the entrance from under the mezzanine offers a whimsical 'Englishness' with garden gnomes and a shed of studied dilapidation in the courtyard.

MIDDLE RIGHT

On the second and third floors a social space, in front of the stairs and lifts, looks over the glazed roof of the new structure.

BOTTOM LEFT

Ground Floor Plan
1 Entrance
2 Void
3 Reception
4 Terrace
5 Studio
6 VIP room
7 Meeting room
8 Kitchen
9 Lavatories
10 Stair
11 Lift
12 Lavatories

BOTTOM RIGHT

First Floor Plan
1 Mezzanine social area
2 Void
3 Meeting room
4 Storage
5 Lockers
6 Lavatories
7 Stair
8 Lift

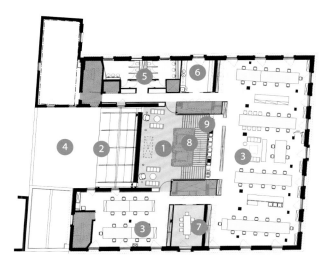

GROUND FLOOR PLAN, SCALE 1:300

FIRST FLOOR PLAN, SCALE 1:300

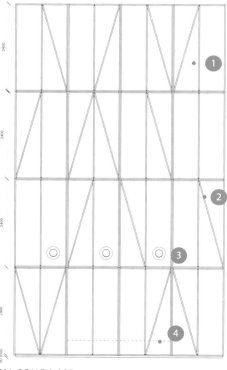

ELEVATION, SCALE 1:100

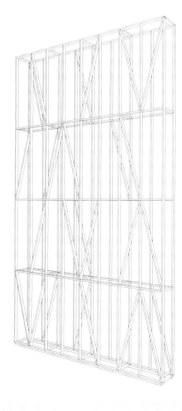

ABOVE
The three-dimensional tracery of the 'Folly' structure, with its ostensibly carelessly placed letters of Mulberry in different fonts, connects the basement ground and first floors.

FAR LEFT
'Folly' Structure
1 Painted acoustic board lining on back of frame
2 Clear sealed 96x32mm (3¾ x1¼ in) wooden framing
3 Air supply nozzles set flush with face of acoustic board
4 Air extract grill painted to match acoustic board

LEFT
The sealed natural plywood block of the 'folly' structure.

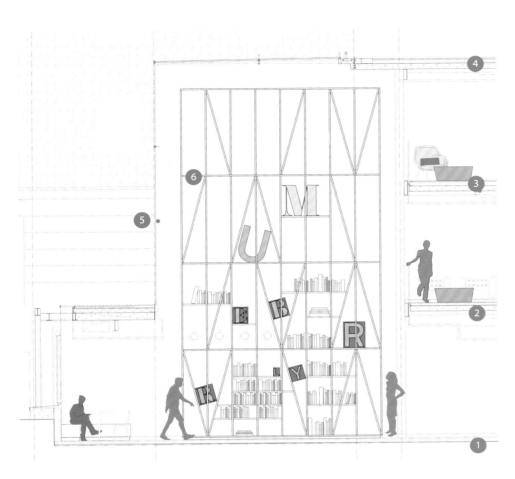

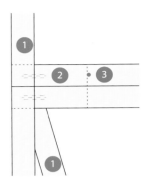

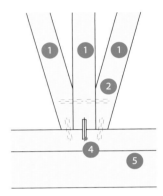

ELEVATION, SCALE 1:100

DETAIL, SCALE 1:5

ABOVE
Section Through New Structure
1 Basement level
2 Ground floor
3 First floor
4 Second floor

5 New glazed steel framed structure
6 'Folly' wall

TOP RIGHT
'Folly' Wall Joints
1 96 x 32mm (3¾ x1¼ in) timber framing

2 Biscuit connections
3 Line of half housed joint
4 Dowel connection
5 Base plate

BOTTOM LEFT AND RIGHT
In studio spaces worktables are punctuated by informal discussion places. Walls are hung with material samples and visual research material.

VANACHAI, BANGKOK
OPENBOX CO. LTD.

Vanachai means 'victory in saving forests' in Thai and the name indicates the environmental priorities of a company, established in 1943, that is one of the largest manufacturers of particle boards in Asia. It was important that its new headquarters building should reflect its philosophy and introduce its established credentials to potential customers who increasingly share its principles. The designers visited its factories looking for aspects of the production processes that might be reinterpreted in the new building.

The footprint of the new building filled the site as comprehensively as the regulation setbacks allowed and the triangular geometry led naturally to a spectacular massing that would have been otherwise difficult to justify. The drama was heightened when an open air, triple-height arrival hall was created at the sharpest point of the triangle. The escalator from ground level arrives at the bottom of the enclosed atrium in a metal-framed glazed box and its passengers enter a four storey volume under the soffits of flights of shallow pitched stairs. The designers decided that if the company's products were to be displayed in the building then it would be more effective if all were to be concentrated in the atrium, which offered scope for spectacle. In the office areas there is very little effort to use products other than as flooring, where it makes strictly practical good sense.

The stairs slice through and twist in the volume of the atrium and from above or below make a complex layering of monolithic planes. Soffits are smooth, balustrades are wide and all are clad in timber the colour and grain of which contrast with the smooth white concrete edge beams of the floor slabs. A very gentle pitch elongates the length of each flight and the inclined planes of the balustrades, with parallel top and bottom edges, give no hint of the steps they conceal. Joints in the boarding are at right angles to the top and bottom edges, which expresses the flights as horizontal elements angled to span directly between lower levels. The designers compare them to tree trunks, casually stacked after felling. At upper levels they rest on and wrap around the single concrete column that rises through the void. Placement of windows means that direct sunlight only penetrates the atrium in late afternoon to cast shadows on and from the stairs, mimicking the patterns of natural light in the forest at the end of the day.

TOP
An escalator carries pedestrians from street level to the base of the atrium. Vertical sheeting clads the car parking levels.

MIDDLE
The building plan replicates the angles of the site.

BOTTOM
The stair planes show clearly against the regular geometry of the façade.

TOP LEFT
The escalator arrives at atrium level in a glazed box. Wide flights of stone steps lead to the base of the timber-clad stairs.

TOP RIGHT
The escalator climbs through a tunnel lined with Vanachai products.

MIDDLE LEFT
Mitred junctions and seemingly unbroken balustrade planes suggest solidity and celebrate the texture of timber.

MIDDLE RIGHT
Gentle gradients elongate the flights, which seem to rest lightly on the floors they connect.

BOTTOM
Section
1 Exterior escalator
2 Internal escalator
3 Atrium
4 Stair
5 Carpark ramp
6 Car parking
7 Office floor

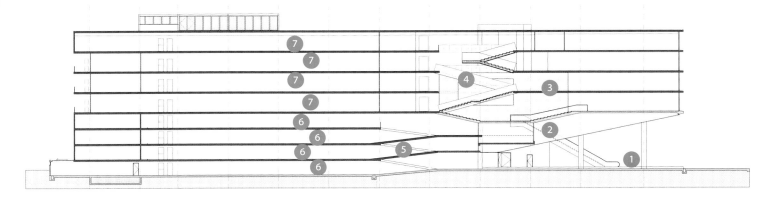

SECTION, SCALE 1:500

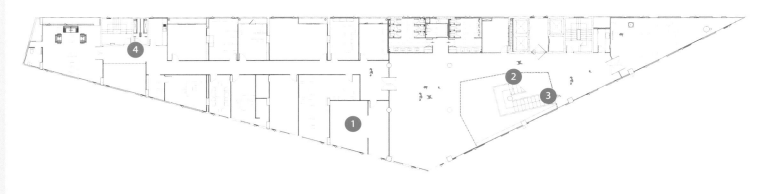

EIGHTH FLOOR PLAN, SCALE 1:500

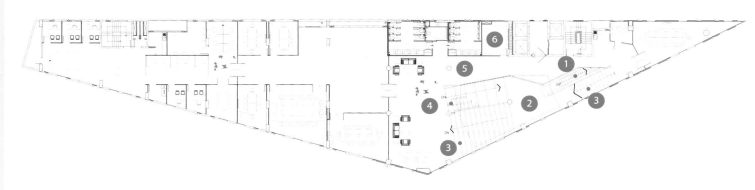

FIFTH FLOOR PLAN, SCALE 1:500

TOP
Eighth Floor Plan
1 Void
2 Stair down
3 Stair up
4 Lift lobby

MIDDLE
Fifth Floor Plan
1 Escalator from street level
2 Lower atrium floor
3 Stone stairs to upper atrium level
4 Upper atrium floor level
5 Stair to upper floors
6 Lift lobby

BOTTOM
On the office floors, exposed service
conduit panel joints and fixings provide
a raw industrial context for a wall
decoration of a sliced and sectioned
tree trunk. Only the floor promotes a
company product.

TOP LEFT
Views through the stairwell present complex compositions of heavy timber planes.

TOP RIGHT
Gentle gradients allow the individual flights to make a relaxed occupation of the atrium void, asserting their significance.

BOTTOM
Apart from the flooring and plywood chair shells, which might be found in any office interior, finishes in the canteen reject product placement.

SKYPE,
STOCKHOLM
PS ARKITECKTUR

It is seldom that the identity of a company or its activity can be or should be expressed with sharp specificity, but for this project, located in the shell of an old brewery and providing audio and video studios, workplaces for up to one hundred people, meeting rooms and social spaces, the designers tackled head on the task of giving tangible expression to something as intangible as digital connectivity. Their strategy was to express, with artefacts of two and three dimensions, the idea of an interconnected world in general and the client's iconography in particular.

The existing fabric of the building is treated casually, painted white to neutralise irregularities and idiosyncrasies. Other colours evolve from company graphics. The blue of the logo appears in the upholstery of a few of the globular chairs in the entrance space and is the reference for subsequent colour choices. There are no dramatic spatial gestures. Creative effort is concentrated on the generation of surface pattern and complementary furniture pieces.

In the most abstract interpretation connectivity is distilled to a pattern of triangles, in four shades of grey, for the bespoke carpet and, most literally, in the motifs of cables and headphones used in the digitally printed, project specific wallpapers. Digital printing permits not only multiple variations on themes but location-specific modifications, as in the local adaptations of repeat patterns that frame a screen and in the harmonising, however raucous, of wallpaper and carpet colours. Three-dimensional expressions of themes relate to, and gain from their affinity with, two-dimensional equivalents. The stretched triangular legs of the high tables, designated for informal social or professional interaction obviously relate to the triangular carpet pattern. Lighting tubes hanging at angles also pick up the rhythm of the carpet pattern. Bulbous chairs and clusters of spherical white light fittings suggest the cartoonish clouds of the company logo.

Whimsy is evident throughout. Small light fittings, too small to contribute significantly to general illumination, are spaced along the length of graphic cables, implying that power is drawn from them rather than from sources within the wall and the cables become fronds of vegetation with headphones for flower heads. When real cables carry power to real bulbs they also serve a graphic function, spelling out Skype in a reasonable approximation of the company logo or tracing the carpet's triangular pattern against wall panels painted in the carpet's grey tones.

RIGHT
Internet connectivity inspires the pattern of the bespoke carpet and is expressed three dimensionally in the high tables. The bulbous shapes of upholstered chairs refer to the clouds of the logo.

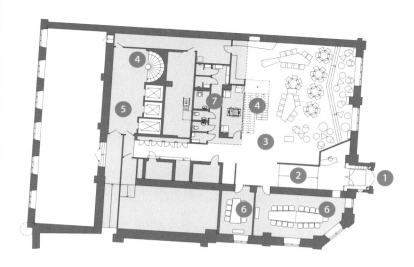

LOWER FLOOR PLAN, SCALE 1:400

UPPER FLOOR PLAN, SCALE 1:400

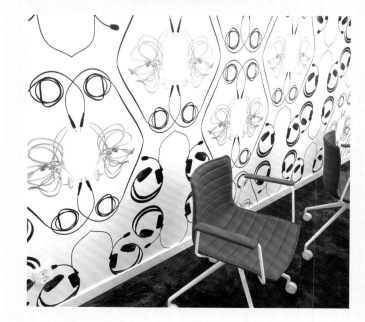

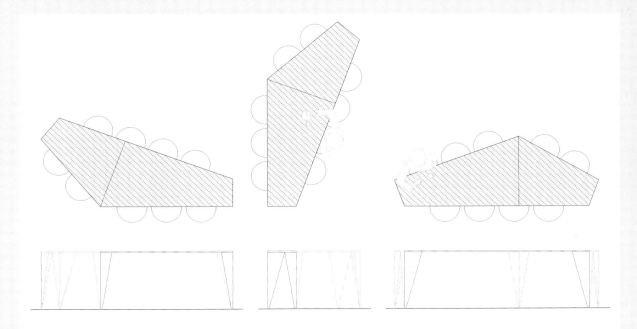

OPPOSITE TOP LEFT

Lower Floor Plan

1 Entrance
2 Ramp
3 Double height social area
4 Stair
5 Lifts
6 Meeting room
7 Lavatories

OPPOSITE BOTTOM LEFT

Upper Floor Plan

1 Stair
2 Lifts
3 Work stations
4 Casual meeting table
5 Meeting room
6 Social area
7 Lavatories

OPPOSITE TOP RIGHT

Coloured wires can harmonise with upholstery fabric and carpet colours and their extravagant loops leave no doubt that they are a decorative device.

OPPOSITE MIDDLE RIGHT

Bespoke production allows wallpaper patterns to be created for very particular locations.

OPPOSITE BOTTOM RIGHT

Custom designed wallpaper patterns draw on the headphones and wires of digital communication.

TOP

The plan of the table top and the elevation of its legs evolve from the same source as the triangular carpet pattern. When grouped they determine a more casual social interaction.

RIGHT

Clustered translucent spheres of pendant lights also interpret the logo clouds. The glazed wall of the meeting room above the kitchen lends some of the colourful complexity of the work floors to the major social space.

LEFT
The zigzagging coloured wire is the crucial component in this decorated wall. The lightbulb, casually off centre in the dark grey block, plays with the idea of function.

BOTTOM LEFT
Digital devices can evolve graphically, while the small light fitting in the top right stubbornly implies that the printed line is a live wire.

BOTTOM RIGHT
As an alternative to wires and headphones, images of computer keys break up the plane of a flat white wall.

RIGHT
An electric cable, fixed by standard plastic clips, makes a complicated detour between a power socket and the deliberately modest light fitting it feeds, to trace a facsimile of the company logo.

BOTTOM LEFT
Lighting tubes are hung at angles to complement the carpet pattern. The thick grey curtain helps acoustics.

BOTTOM RIGHT
The visual fussiness of white cable on white wall, sometimes doubled by shadows cast by sections hanging loose, complements that of the tracery of white chairs and stools.

BARCODE,
SINGAPORE
MINISTRY OF DESIGN

In creating their own workplace Ministry of Design applied the principles that underpin all their work: a response to physical context, a rigorously edited material and colour palette and well honed conceptual thinking that permeates all practical decision making. The shell, on the top floor of what were formerly six shop units at the intersection of Singapore's central business district and its historic Chinatown, met the practice's ambition to accommodate all staff and facilities on one level, encouraging communication and interaction and eroding hierarchical barriers. The single floor is conceived as a series of distinct functional spaces that lie within boundaries established by black floored perimeter circulation zones. The strictly regular lengths and irregular widths on plan of a dedicated work area, formal and informal meeting places, discussion zones and a retreat room establish a linear diagram that gives the interior its 'Barcode' soubriquet. The diagram is reinforced by the white communal work tables that stretch the full width of the studio and by the table that stretches the full length of the conference room so that separate sliding doors are necessary to give access to each side. The mirror-clad end wall doubles the table's length so that it makes the division appear even more formidable as it disappears into the reflected gloom.

Opposite the entrance, in the 'gallery' with its stepped seating, the company has its amphitheatre, which presents an ambiguous and challenging face to visiting clients and gives staff space to debate and experiment. Smaller auxiliary spaces are located along the existing entrance wall to absorb the irregularities of its plan and present a more ordered face to the studio. The dedicated areas within the central zone are designed to be visually separate but all conform to the black and white palette. That rule is relaxed in the auxiliary spaces where the natural timber cladding of the library offers an organic retreat from the bright white hard-edged work spaces and in the small meeting room which flaunts curves and soft red finishes for those hungry for colour and upholstery. While these marginal spaces represent the most radical departures from conceptual principles there are details, like the mirror ball and its reflected spots of light which dapple the white surfaces, and the question and exclamation marks on the meeting room's black walls that exhort participants to think and contribute. These details lighten the mood throughout the central zone and are the more effective because they frivolously complement the grander, more sombre gestures.

TOP
A black recessed entrance frames the white interior.

BOTTOM
The 'gallery', a multi-use space, sits opposite the entrance and immediately confounds visitors' expectations about a reception space. Each step is 480mm high, perfect for sitting and challenging to ascend.

OPPOSITE
Spots of light reflected off a slowly rotating mirror ball animate the white planes. A secluded corner becomes a meeting space.

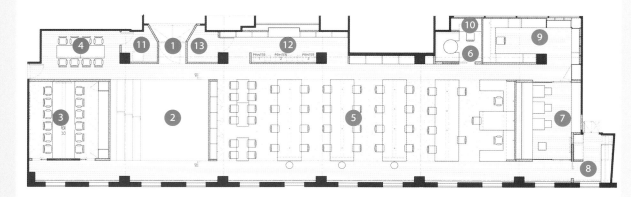

PLAN, SCALE 1:250

TOP
Prompted by the barcode image the white conference table runs from wall to wall, floating between the dark, acoustically deadened floor, walls and ceiling. Each side of the table is accessed through its own door.

MIDDLE
The white studio worktables, on the black timber boarded floor, consolidate the barcode concept and, like the conference table, stretch to the permitted limits of the zone, here defined by the black wall to the gallery space and the black floors of the circulation zones.

BOTTOM
Plan
1 Entrance
2 Gallery
3 Conference room
4 Meeting room 1
5 Studio
6 Discussion area
7 Play room
8 Pantry
9 Material library
10 Meeting room 2
11 Storage
12 Material library and printing area
13 Server room

OPPOSITE TOP LEFT
The 'hot desk' discussion area represents a minor infringement of the barcode diagram. The three tables set parallel to the long axis of the room float visually above the lower surface that does obey the formula. The red interior in the background deviates from the black and white palette and is a second breach.

OPPOSITE TOP RIGHT
In the smallest meeting room red floor, wall and ceiling finishes and a multi-coloured image provide sanctuary from black and white.

OPPOSITE BOTTOM
The barcode sequence ends in a 'play' room in which staff may relax, think and discuss. Sliding doors provide a measure of acoustic isolation. The natural timber flooring suggests somewhere perhaps more domestic.

BERGEN INTERNATIONAL FESTIVAL, BERGEN
ERIKSEN SKAJAA ARKITEKTER AS

The Bergen International Festival, founded in 1953, is an important annual musical and cultural event. Performances take place in concert halls, the former homes of local composers, churches, streets and squares. The festival's offices were formerly housed in rooms within an old bank building but it was decided that, because of a move towards project based work, its new premises should be open plan. The pattern of usage changes throughout the year with a shift from the planning period to the time of the festival itself when both the nature of activity and the number of workers increases significantly.

For the new interior the designers aimed not only for flexibility of work spaces but also proposed that it should be capable of hosting small concerts and exhibitions. They conceived the offices as workshops in which the festival would be made and as the back of house, supporting the public performances. This concept found expression in a collection of wooden framed pieces, the basic elements of division and enclosure. Though made with great precision it was important that these elements should appear incomplete and capable of adaptation. When spaces are enclosed framing for glazing sits behind the uprights and from the outside the structure continues to appear skeletal and open. To consolidate the sense of impermanence recessed base and head plates suggest that frames touch neither floor nor ceiling while the corner junction implies neither overlap nor connection between abutting lengths.

During planning those rooms that were necessarily permanent were positioned to support most effectively the options offered by flexibility. On the lower floor two flexible spaces may be used as a project office or a dining room and the latter may be closed off with sections of movable wall for use as a concert hall, with a stage set against the stair core, or a grand piano located against the unglazed external wall. On the upper floor permanent rooms and the newly enclosed stairwell set up two open plan office areas. A meeting room doubles as a place for temporary workers.

The material palette is simple with a Scandinavian appetite for birch, which is used for the framing pieces and those rooms with visible framing have birch ceilings and floors. Otherwise floors are polished concrete. Plastered walls are painted black or white with shadow gap skirtings and in those rooms ceilings are plastered. The original nonagonal stair is encased in a mutation of the standard grid which becomes a birch veneered zone of shelves, cabinets, benches, and a niche for the bronze bust of the festival's founder, the singer Fanny Elster.

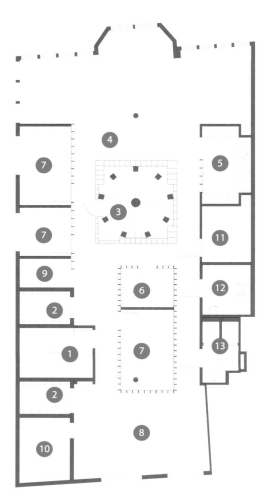

FIFTH FLOOR PLAN, SCALE 1:200

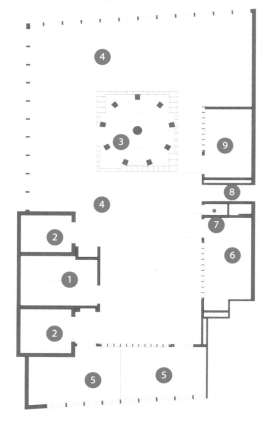

SIXTH FLOOR PLAN, SCALE 1:200

RIGHT

New partitions around the meeting room on the fifth floor illustrate the principles of the system, the corner junction, the shadow gaps at top and bottom and the plywood and glass infill panels set on inner faces.

BOTTOM LEFT

Meeting and Print Rooms
The regular rhythm of the vertical birch framing supports plywood and glass infill panels which in turn provide lateral stability.

BOTTOM RIGHT

Exposed framing brings depth and texture to normally bland corridor walls.

LEFT
Internal stair: The original nine-sided enclosure is wrapped in the new birch framed structure. The deeper volumes created on the corners of the square are exploited for storage, seating and entrance.

BOTTOM
Space dividers: Dividers are mobile (types 1, 2 and 3) on wheels with low level storage to add stability and angled braces to increase stability or permanent (types 4 and 5) fixed at floor and ceiling.

ABOVE
The regular rhythm of the vertical framing members, here around the stair, can be varied for practical and aesthetic ends. The simple structure of the trestle table complements that of the partitions.

OPPOSITE
The areas between the original stair and the corners of the new square frame allow the insertion of deeper elements but the basic vertical rhythm remains clear.

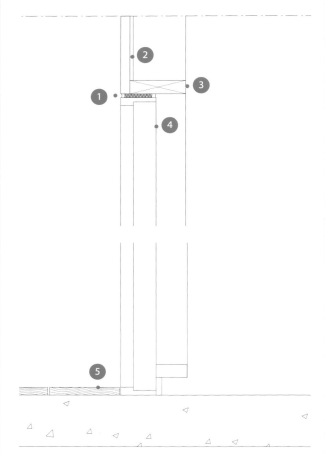

SECTION, SCALE 1:5

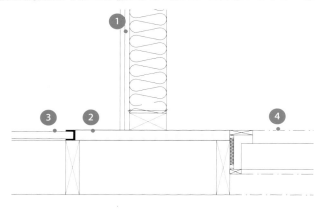

PLAN, SCALE 1:5

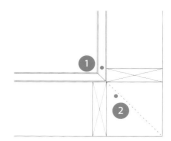

PLAN, SCALE 1:5

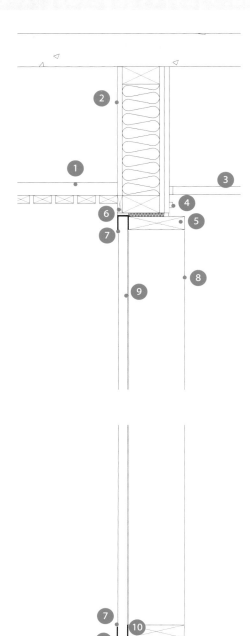

SECTION, SCALE 1:5

PLAN, SCALE 1:5

TOP LEFT
Section Detail: Door
1 Joint recess painted to match wall
2 27mm (1 in) white stained birch veneered plywood
3 36x148mm (1⅜ x 6 in) white stained birch stud
4 Door leaf
5 21x185mm (⅞ x 7¼ in) birch flooring

TOP RIGHT
Section Detail: Glass Partition
1 Suspended ceiling with 10mm (⅜ in) gap between birch slats
2 2 layers of 12.5mm (½ in) plasterboard with noise reducing insulation quilt
3 Ceiling
4 LED strip with white light
5 White stained 36x148mm (1⅜ x 6 in) birch stud
6 13x48mm (½in x 2 in) smooth planed birch
7 40mm (1½ in) profile by glass supplier
8 Vertical birch stud behind
9 Sound reducing glass
10 Packing piece
11 48x98mm (2 x 4 in) birch sill
12 13x48mm (½in x 2 in) smooth birch

MIDDLE
Plan Detail: Junction of Glass Panel, Door and Partition
1 2 layers of 12.5mm (½ in) plasterboard with noise reducing insulation quilt on 98mm(4 in) studs
2 24mm (1 in) birch veneered plywood flush with aluminium frame section
3 Glass in aluminium frame
4 Line of birch door frame

BOTTOM LEFT
Plan Detail: Corner
1 Silicon corner seal
2 Horizontal bottom stud
3 Vertical stud

BOTTOM RIGHT
Plan Detail: Junction of Door and Glass Panel
1 Birch door frame and leaf
2 Recessed junction between door frame and aluminium glass frame
3 Aluminium glass frame
4 Sound reducing glass
5 Stud framing tight against glass

TOP LEFT
The basic unit, the skeleton of the stud frame, performs as a screen to the kitchen area on the fifth floor.

TOP RIGHT
Existing elements are painted black or white and provide a contrasting backdrop for the new birch structures and furniture in the shared office on the upper floor.

RIGHT
In glazed sections new frames sit in front of, and take precedence over, the end of existing partitions.

GOLDBERGER, BUDAPEST
TERVHIVATAL

Within the five metre high floor of this former textile factory an internet and graphic advertising design company required separate places to house their different activities. They expressed their aversion to the bland honeycomb of standard office cubicles and further complicated the brief with their eccentric request for a workplace that might double as a night club.

The designers' solution was to deconstruct the honeycomb and place a number of free-standing, steel-framed, plasterboard-clad 'boxes' across the generous three hundred square metres of floor area, which easily accommodated the extravagant areas dedicated to circulation and separation. The solution was also apposite because, without being unduly literal, it relates to the client's rotating cube logo. The boxes house a reception area opposite the entrance, a manager's office, a small meeting room and a larger meeting space with kitchen and service counter that is capable of supporting the nocturnal club activities. Their smooth white planes, which contrast with the rougher curved soffits of the existing floor structure above them, are incised with thin, angled lines that snake across and disturb their otherwise uneventful rectangular surfaces. Each box is slightly elevated to underline its implied status as a discrete entity and the spaces between them become corridors. Metal tread plate is folded to create steps at each door position and laid flat to cover a length of raised corridor between the reception box and the small meeting room. When the office assumes its alter ego and becomes a club LED lights, concealed in the recessed plinths of boxes, wash across the existing floor to reinforce the idea of floating boxes and across the existing ceiling to emphasise its textures and geometry. Other existing elements, the original windows and vaulted niches, are retained as counterpoints to the precision of the new. The grey linoleum floors within the boxes sits comfortably with the polished concrete finish of the base floor level. The loose white pebbles that fill the floor recesses for plumbing pipes and electrical cables provide contrasting texture.

The design period was necessarily brief and construction details were evolved on site in collaboration with the contractors. Wanda Reich and Noemi Varga were responsible for fitting out the interiors of the boxes and adopted and adapted the idea of the floating box to make a hanging desk, suspended from the ceiling and stabilised by connections to the adjacent wall.

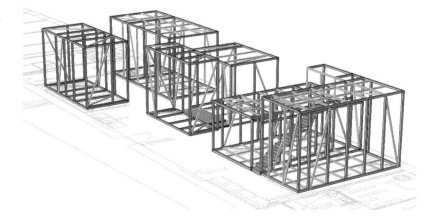

TOP
The reception cube, directly opposite the entrance, states the interior's theme of free-standing cuboids, visually free of floor and ceiling. A glass counter top and front panel open up views to other cubes.

BOTTOM
'Box' framing diagram
Angled struts provide lateral stability.

TOP LEFT
During the day the blocks dramatise the effect of natural light, the intensely bright white of directly lit planes against deep shade and between them the gentler washing of the polished concrete floor and the rippling profiles of the ceiling slab.

TOP RIGHT
A line wraps across a window, round a corner and across the door to the kitchen.

RIGHT
At night lights above the recessed plinth further isolate boxes and floor and add night club glamour. High level lighting accentuates the pattern of the ceiling structure.

TOP
At night the office meeting room with its bar servery comfortably assumes its identity as a club, even before lighting effects add drama. The folded tread plate steps read as clearly separate white wall and concrete floor, reinforcing the visual independence of both.

LEFT
The flat planes of the box exteriors are relieved by incised black lines and the smooth sheen of the floor by the pebbles that cover the plumbing pipes and electrical cable that run in perimeter recesses.

OPPOSITE TOP LEFT
In the corridor between reception and small meeting room, too narrow for individual steps, the floor level is raised to that of the box interiors, finished in tread plate, with two steps at each end.

OPPOSITE TOP RIGHT
The hanging desk offers another interpretation of the floating cube. The wall next to it can give it the stability that the suspension wires cannot.

OPPOSITE BOTTOM
Plan
1 Entrance
2 Reception
3 Meeting/social/club area
4 Bar servery
5 Private office
6 Small meeting room
7 Shared offices
8 Lavatory
9 Kitchen
10 Storage

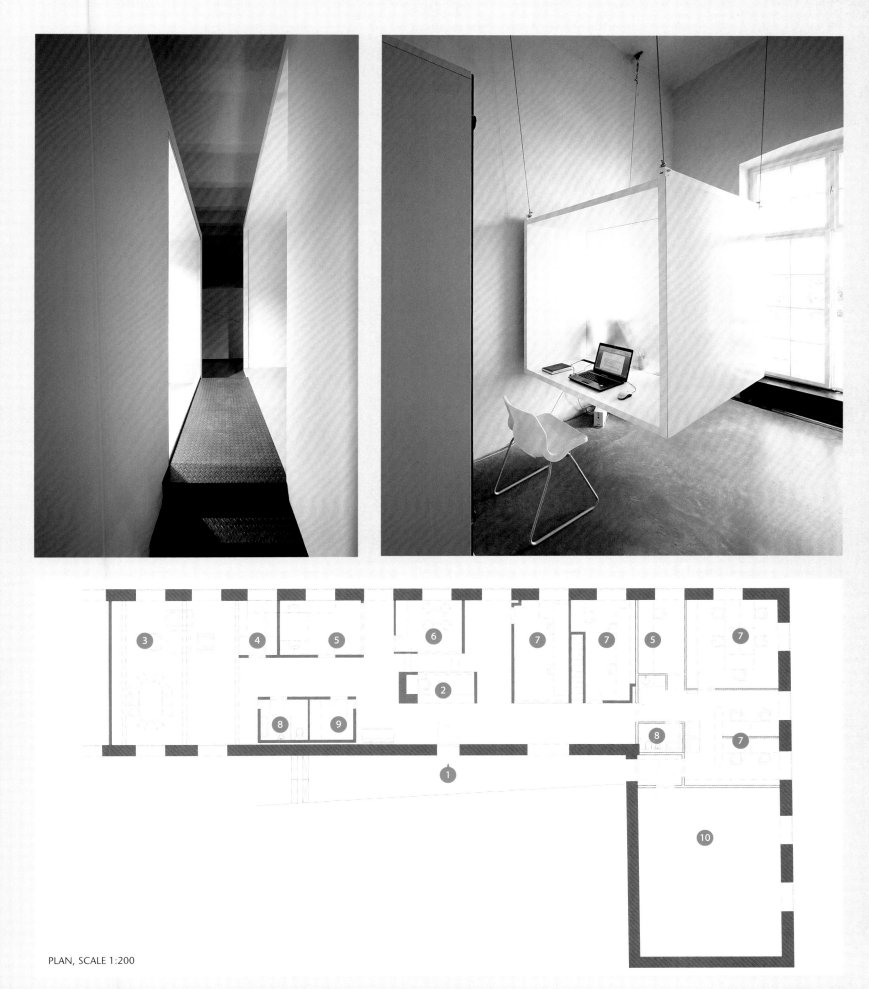

PLAN, SCALE 1:200

KAWANISHI FAM, KURASHIKI
TT ARCHITECTS

This former coffee roasting warehouse has been converted into a flexible work place for emerging entrepreneurs. It subscribes to the idea that creativity is nurtured by collaboration and interaction and offers an environment of shared desks and a shared meeting room in which those who would normally work alone have the opportunity to share experiences, to discuss problems and offer solutions, to put in perspective the anxieties that afflict and distract those who work in isolation.

The interior has been stripped of evidence of bias towards a particular business model or activity. Its aesthetic emerges from a rational and elemental expression of the architectonic qualities that are inherent in the existing building. It demonstrates an underlying logic that will insinuate itself, however subliminally, into users' psyches and which complements the methodical and objective thinking that is necessary to develop a business idea, however spontaneously it might have been conceived. It also offers for consideration a clearly expressed concept that will engage entrepreneurs' wandering minds in gentle speculation that will nurture the mechanics of rational critical thinking.

The building shell lends itself to clarity of expression. Its forty-five degree roof pitch makes a diagrammatic section that corresponds to an instinctive perception of building form. The geometric perfection of the section is consolidated by the elevation of the timber clad 'hut' containing utilities and lavatory which is stripped of complexities. The entrance to utilities has neither door leaf nor frame and the essential door to the lavatory is invisible from the work space. The framing of the glazed screen between work space and meeting room, which matches the cladding of the 'hut', stops at window head height, allowing the ceiling, and the light fittings suspended from it, to run uninterrupted between the principal spaces. It provides just enough separation to give privacy to hushed voices. A pair of concrete columns marks the midpoint of the total volume and the windows and the rooflights above them establish symmetry. The windows' traditional fenestration pattern emphasises the restraint of all other elements.

TOP
The precise geometry of ceiling and rooflights set the precedent for this obsessively rational environment, an incubator in which fledgling entrepreneurs may interact and flourish.

BOTTOM
Cross section
1 Timber-framed glazed screen
2 Utility room/lavatory 'hut'

SECTION, SCALE 1:75

TOP LEFT

The timber-framed clear glass screen between meeting room and work space stops at window head height and is there to mark territory rather provide total privacy.

TOP RIGHT

The 'hut' that contains a lavatory and utility room locks precisely into the strict geometry of the building's section. Its timber cladding balances that of the glazed screen at the other end of the space and the omission of a door leaf is prompted by the same reductive impulse that stops the screen short of the ceiling.

MIDDLE LEFT

A single concrete column breaks the perfect whiteness of the side walls, makes a link with the tints and textures of the timber elements and provides the reference point for the symmetrical organisation of windows and rooflights.

BOTTOM
Plan
1 Entrance lobby
2 Lift
3 Stair
4 Work space
5 Meeting room
6 Utility room
7 Lavatory

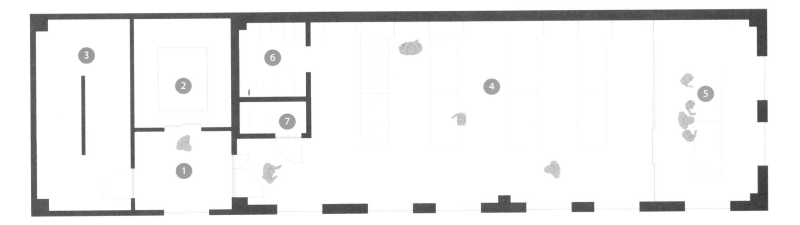

PLAN, SCALE 1:100

NO PICNIC, STOCKHOLM
ELDING OSCARSON

For their new studio No Picnic, a large multi-disciplinary design practice, found two nineteenth century buildings in Stockholm, one originally an exercise hall for soldiers and the other a stable for police horses, that broadly met their needs. Although the historical importance of the two had earned them protected status, both had been roughly treated by earlier conversions. The designers decided to strip both buildings back to their structural essence and were able to do this easily in the stable where their only addition, apart from furniture, was a bespoke, quilted, acoustic lining to the lower walls.

In the exercise hall it was necessary, for function and economy, to retain a mezzanine from the 80s but, like so many apparent obstacles, this became the catalyst for the creation of the element that subsequently defined the whole interior. The designers regretted how the mezzanine, which ran the length of the hall, along its centre line, interfered with the original simple and symmetrical volume. They constructed a 4 metres high wall along its face that they clad in a skin of polished aluminium sheet, mounted on sheets of laminated plywood and capable of accurately reflecting the double height volume of the unaltered half of the room. The wall was high enough to enclose the space under the mezzanine and to project above it to form a balustrade to the balcony that gave access to the project rooms on the upper level. Rooms at the lower level had no windows in their external wall and consequently borrowed light from the double-height space through large rectangles of clear laminated glass set in the aluminium. These also reflected the windows in the external wall opposite.

The image in the glass appears to be that in a mirror and the precision of the reflection in the aluminium suggests it is the reality. The trompe l'oeil is accentuated by the thinness of the wall, revealed at the edges of the glass panels, which suggests it may be a mirror, and by the aluminium panel that separates glass from floor and further confuses the relationship of the rooms visible through the glass to the 'real' interior implied in the reflection. The two staircases work in their different ways with the reflecting wall. The spiral becomes a single symmetrical abstraction and the straight flight appears to be a distinct pair. Both add to the visual conundrum.

TOP
The simple solidity of the traditional rendered exterior gives no hint of the ambiguous, fragile and layered interior.

BOTTOM
The aluminium wall hides the mezzanine, doubles the perceived volume and offers an imprecise parallel world. The conventional spiral stair becomes an unfamiliar and extraordinary object.

OPPOSITE TOP
Polished aluminium panels that run along the central axis of the double-height central space act as mirrors and reflect the opposite external wall. Clear glass panels let light into meeting rooms and produce a softer and slightly misaligned image.

OPPOSITE BOTTOM LEFT
Ground floor plan

1 Entrance
2 Reception and lobby
3 Polished aluminium/glass wall
4 Meeting rooms
5 Prototyping
6 Spiral stair
7 Straight stair
8 Canteen
9 Services
10 Studio

OPPOSITE BOTTOM RIGHT
First Floor Plan
1 Spiral stair
2 Straight stair
3 Voids above lobby and canteen
4 Polished aluminium wall as balustrade
5 Meeting rooms
6 Clients' private meeting room
7 Informal meeting area
8 Studio

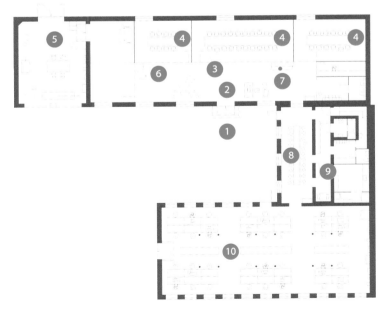

GROUND FLOOR PLAN, SCALE 1:400

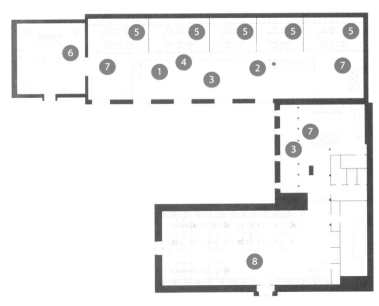

FIRST FLOOR PLAN, SCALE 1:400

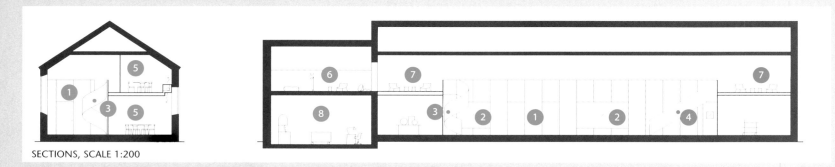

SECTIONS, SCALE 1:200

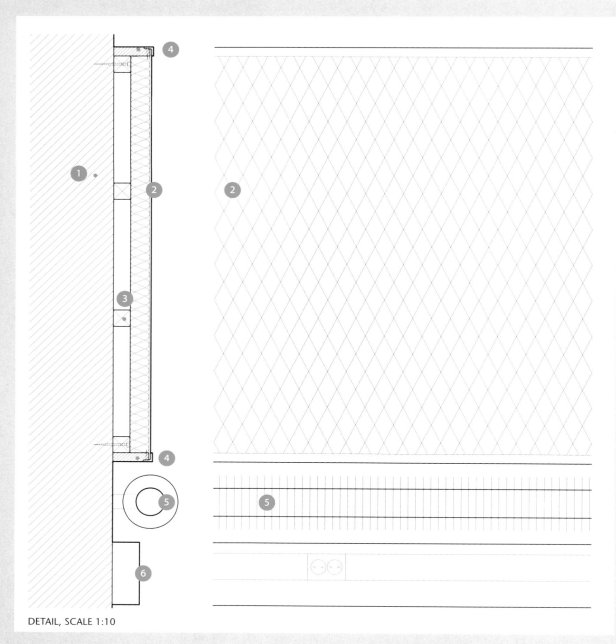

DETAIL, SCALE 1:10

TOP

Sections
1 Polished aluminium wall
2 Glass section
3 Spiral stair
4 Straight stair
5 Meeting room
6 Clients' private meeting room
7 Informal meeting area
8 Prototyping

MIDDLE

Detail: Sound Insulation
1 Existing wall
2 Quilted insulation
3 Timber fixing batten screwed to wall
4 Painted timber batten
5 Perimeter finned heating pipe
6 Perimeter wiring conduit

BOTTOM

Detail: Polished aluminium and glass wall
1 Birch plywood
2 Untreated plywood face to meeting rooms
3 Loose tongue gap joint
4 3mm (⅛ in) rolled aluminium sheet sandwich
5 Untreated plywood edge
6 8mm (⅜ in) laminated glass fixed with silicon tape
7 Plywood rebated for flush glazing
8 Rebated edge to concealed door
9 9mm (⅜ in) birch plywood door face on timber frame
10 Concealed hinge
11 Polished aluminium door handle

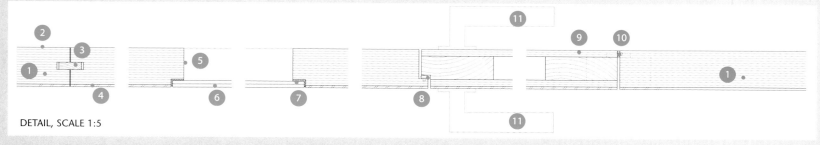

DETAIL, SCALE 1:5

TOP LEFT

The reflecting wall appears to slide between the two manifestations of the straight stair. The walls that divide meeting rooms on the mezzanine floor sit far enough back from the mirrored balustrade to be inconspicuous at entrance level.

ABOVE LEFT

The lower walls of the main studio are lined with quilted felt to improve acoustics.

TOP RIGHT

The top of the table in the staff canteen is halved – like the principal space beyond.

RIGHT

The window opening reveals a surprisingly thin and apparently delicate division between lobby and meeting rooms. The mirrored section beneath the window makes the stronger reflection in the aluminium dominant. The lobby chairs appear to float, like ghosts, in the meeting room and contrast with the truer reflection in the open, aluminium clad, door although that in its turn creates further optical confusion.

ONESIZE, AMSTERDAM
ORIGINS ARCHITECTS

OneSize is a motion graphics design company and their new office space offers another persuasive example of how redundant industrial buildings adapt particularly well to providing both the practical necessities and the less tangible qualities that make an inspiring and productive work place. Free of the low-ceilinged, ribbon-windowed modularity of the purpose built office block they exist as self-contained worlds, usually generously proportioned and top lit with no views beyond their own walls, opportunities for designers to set an ambitious agenda.

Origins Architects response to this particular shell is to locate the meeting space and dark rooms, which would more usually be consigned to the perimeter of the plan, at its centre where they become hillocks, which divide and organise the space but, more poetically, also become a plywood landscape. While obviously discrete elements, the three new plywood structures may also be perceived as an entity, with the intersections of the angled planes that crease their side walls lining up to make an explicit connection between the three. While the structures sit on their own terms in the middle of the space, the ribs over the meeting area, which is opposite the entrance, relate easily to the existing roof beams.

Detailing of the elements evolved a close collaboration between the designers and the builders, KNE+, who were appointed early in the project. Much of the speculation and experimentation about detailed construction happened when the work had begun on site and the designers became confident that high fabrication standards would ensure that the complex angled and skewed detailing junctions would be realized with precision. In the finished structures construction details are clear and comprehensible, with lap joints and butt connections visible and easily deciphered. Low grade spruce plywood, normally used for utilitarian construction and hidden behind finishes, is used for both structural and cladding components and, although cost was a consideration in choosing it, the designers believed that the combination of extraordinary objects and inexpensive and familiar materials would be provocatively complementary. The commitment supports the adage that exclusive use of one material enhances construction and, when the material is familiar and mundane, its transformation into extraordinary objects becomes the more impressive.

RIGHT
The sequence of enclosures begins with the freestanding ribs that define the first meeting area. A simple lap joint connects vertical and horizontal components. Intermediate dividing panels at right angles to the long axis of the table give it lateral support.

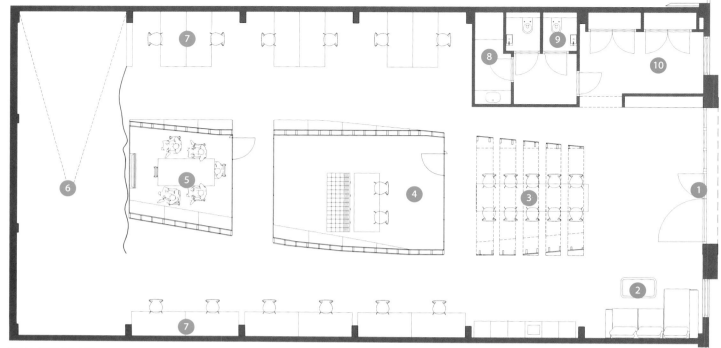

PLAN, SCALE 1:125

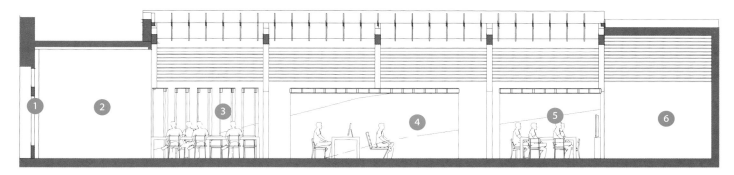

SECTION, SCALE 1:125

OPPOSITE TOP
Plan
1 Entrance
2 Waiting area
3 Ribbed meeting space
4 Small projection room
5 Closed meeting room
6 Large projection space
7 Work stations
8 Shower
9 Lavatory
10 Store

OPPOSITE BOTTOM
The back of the opaque decorated wall acts as a projection screen.

TOP
Section
1 Entrance
2 Waiting area
3 Ribbed meeting space
4 Small projection room
5 Closed meeting room
6 Large projection space

MIDDLE
An opaque decorated wall acts as a screen for projections.

BOTTOM
A single layer of plywood conceals fixings for glazed walls.

TOP LEFT
The layering of opaque, transparent, smooth and textured materials, all complicated by angled planes, sets up rich and ambiguous views.

TOP RIGHT
The plywood ribs take their cue from the concrete roof beams.

BOTTOM
The lamination of plywood edges relates to the patterns of roof joists and fenestration. The geometric logic that determines the profile of the freestanding structures is also applied to desk details.

ABOVE
Plywood structure locks on, visually, to the slightly raised floor of the meeting rooms.

TOP RIGHT
The profiling and angling also shapes tables within the solid walled rooms.

BOTTOM
Rib and wall profiles change in relation to their position in the linear composition that unites the three freestanding enclosures.

RDM, ROTTERDAM
GROSSMAN PARTNERS ARCHITECTEN

RDM originally stood for the initials of Rotterdamsche Droogdog Maatschappij (or Rotterdam Dry Dock Company) but, with the decline of the city's shipbuilding industry, the building that was once the company's head office and dry dock now houses a collaboration between Rotterdam University and the Port of Rotterdam Authority. RDM now stands for Research, Design and Manufacturing. Renamed Innovation Dock, the monumental hall has become a place where students and companies collaborate to produce economic, sustainable solutions for the building, transport and energy industries.

The designers, having organised the existing twenty thousand square metres of floor area with a painted floor grid that defined circulation routes and activity zones, proposed the insertion of an additional floor area seven metres above the existing level and wholly suspended from the gantry tracks that once supported the cranes that serviced the dry dock. Technical data relating to the cranes and their loading capacity provided evidence that the existing structure could comfortably support what is in effect an independent building.

The first unit, of one thousand square metres, is accessed by an external stair and lift, which then connect to other lettable spaces by a system of gangways. New floor areas do not engage with the existing vertical structure, which passes through generous voids between new units that make clear its scale and heavy industrial past. Glimpses of the lime green walls that line the voids and of the interior of the upper level through windows of enormous single sheets of glass indicate the more refined aesthetic of the new. Detailing within the new structure is of a more human scale and finishes are more refined. The unobtrusive suspension system and a light flexible partitioning systems make the reorganising of layouts comparatively simple and more modest volumes make the provision of well-serviced spaces more feasible and more efficient. The space beneath the insertions is high enough to accommodate production processes and events and is dominated by an enormous, sharply detailed satellite image of the port of Rotterdam that wholly covers the soffits of the new floor areas.

RIGHT
The interweaving of new and existing structures was very clear during construction.

OPPOSITE TOP
Sharpness of line and colour set the suspended office structure clearly apart from the collage of heavy engineering components that characterise the old building. The satellite image breaks up what was, potentially, a featureless flat plane. The colours and precision of the painted floor patterns makes a modest connection between old and new.

OPPOSITE BOTTOM
A low-roofed social area, open on two sides but near domestic in scale, hangs like a viewing platform in the monumental volume of the hall. The grid of the metal balustrading is reflected in the padded fabric that clads the remaining two walls. Acidic colour defines the modest space with the mellow tones of existing elements.

LEFT
The complexity of the satellite image has more to do with the intricacy of the existing structure than the diagrammatic precision of the new walls within the voids.

BOTTOM
Plan
1 Existing structure
2 Stair
3 Lift
4 Void
5 Gangway
6 Lettable spaces
7 Access/social area
8 Secondary/escape stair

OPPOSITE TOP
The collage of old structural members and new service ducts that climb through the voids to the existing roof occupies a middle ground between the detail of the satellite image and the simplicity of new elements.

OPPOSITE BOTTOM
Section
1 Lift tower
2 Gangway
3 Stair behind
4 Void
5 Lettable space
6 Secondary/escape stair

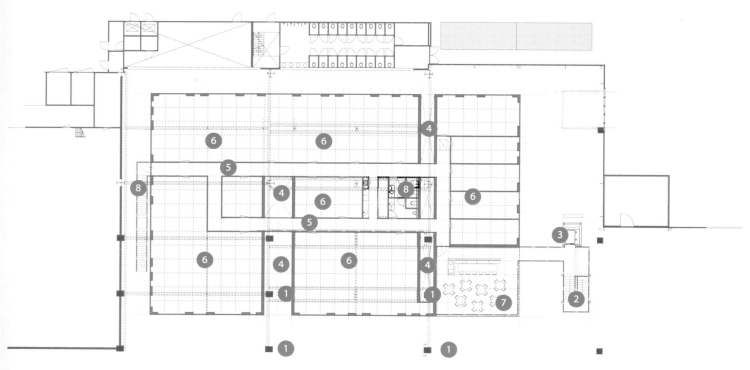

PLAN, SCALE 1:400

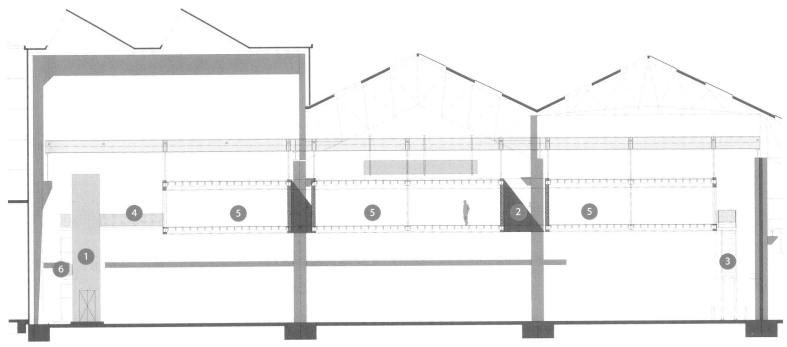

SECTION, SCALE 1:250

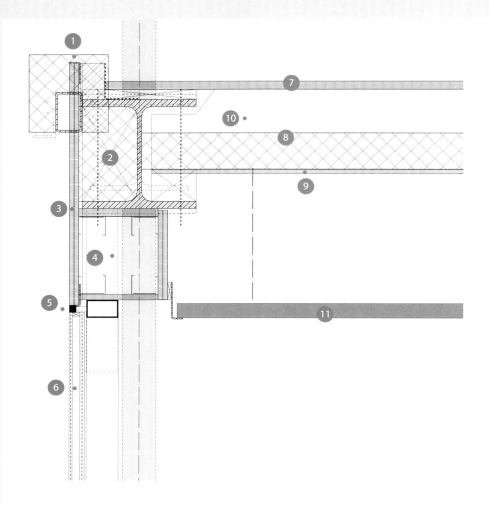

BOTTOM LEFT

Section Through Window Panels
1 Coloured steel frame
2 Mineral wool packing
3 2 layers 12.5mm (½ in) plasterboard
4 Steel hollow section
5 20mm (¾ in) sealant
6 Aluminium glazing frame
7 22mm (⅞ in) plywood decking screwed to timber joists
8 100mm (4 in) mineral wool
9 12.5mm (½ in) plasterboard
10 71x221mm (2¾ x 8½ in) timber joists
11 Proprietary suspended ceiling system
12 Sound insulating glazing
13 Drawbar location
14 Packing piece
15 Laminate floor finish on 30mm (1⅕ in) composite board
16 75x246mm (3 x 9¾ in) timber joists
17 Noise reducing suspended ceiling system

BELOW

Plan: Junction of Window, Solid Panel and Internal Partition
1 2x12.5mm (⅛ x ½ in) composite board
2 100mm (4 in) metal stud
3 Aluminium glazing frame
4 70x70mm (2¾x2¾ in) steel hollow section
5 Mineral wool
6 2x12.5mm (⅛ x ½ in) plasterboard
7 20mm (¾ in) sealant
8 Sound insulating glazed panel

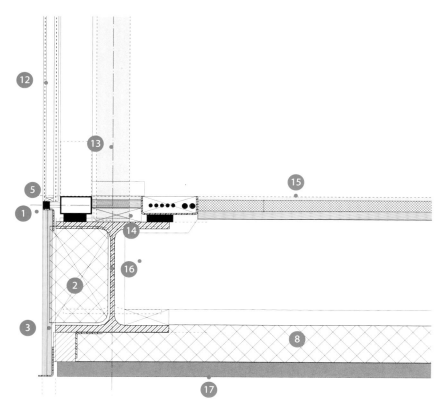

DETAIL, SCALE 1:10

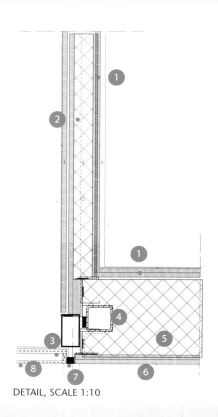

DETAIL, SCALE 1:10

RIGHT

Section

1 Coloured steel frame
2 Mineral wool packing
3 Existing construction
4 2x12.5mm (⅛ x ½ in) plasterboard
5 22mm (⅞ in) plywood
6 22mm (⅞ in) plywood decking screwed to timber joists
7 71x221mm (2¾ x 8½ in) timber joists
8 100mm (4 in) mineral wool
9 12.5mm (½ in)plasterboard
10 Noise reduction suspended ceiling system
11 260mm (10¼ in) metal stud frame
12 Mineral wool
13 2x12.5mm (⅛ x ½ in) composite building board
14 Packing piece
15 Floor duct
16 Laminate floor finish on 30mm (1⅕ in) composite board
17 75x246mm (3 x 9¾ in) timber joist
18 Noise reducing suspended ceiling system

BELOW

Plan: Junction of Internal Position and Window Panel

1 2x12.5mm (⅛ x ½ in) composite board
2 100mm (4 in) metal stud frame
3 Sound insulation seal
4 Film surface on glass closure piece
5 Sound insulating glazed panel

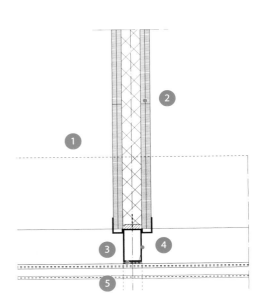

DETAIL, SCALE 1:10

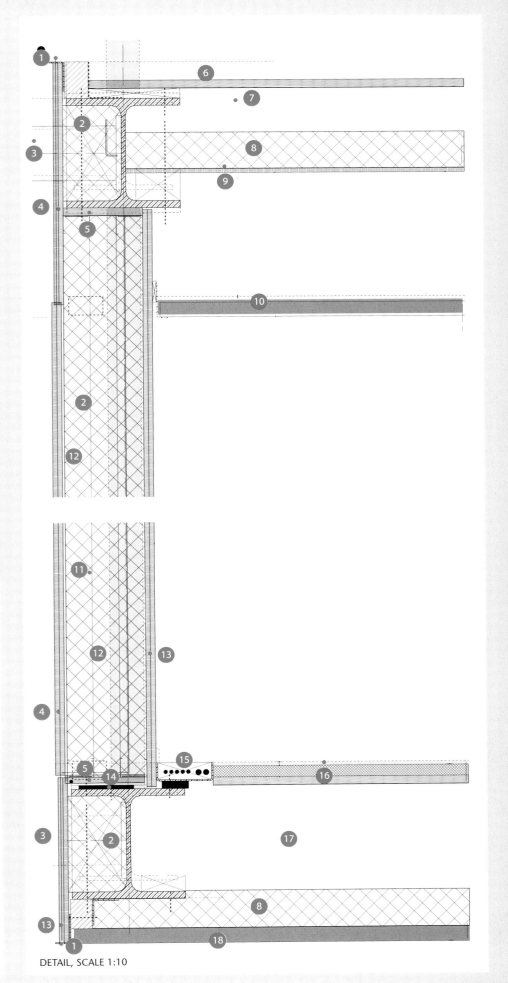

DETAIL, SCALE 1:10

RED BULL, AMSTERDAM
SID LEE ARCHITECTURE

Red Bull's reputation as an enthusiastic patron of extreme sports and radical arts determined the thinking that shaped this project from concept to detailing. The designers persuaded the company to relocate to occupy the three bays of an abandoned single storey factory in a former shipbuilding district, which already boasted a disused Soviet submarine and a concentration of arts and media companies. The new interior with its complex overlapping of public and comparatively private spaces makes an environment that expresses the company's commitment to the symbiosis of social interaction and individual creativity. The tallest of the three bays, which houses the public spaces, is high enough to accommodate, on a mezzanine level, a social space among an undulating landscape of angled roof planes and twisting balustrades. The other two contain shared workstations and managers' offices and meeting rooms. All three sit beneath roof lights that run the length of the building and allow the variations of natural light to play on the writhing geometries. At night strategically deployed and programmed artificial lighting reinterprets the massing.

The most dramatic visual gestures are made in the public area, where chamfered walls and balustrades create a coherent facetted massing into which are inserted dedicated functional spaces. Views to and from the mezzanine further erode any suggestion of conventional rectangularities. The complex geometries of walls and ceiling planes were evolved in close collaboration between the designers and Fiction Factory, the fabricators and builders. The materials, raw and painted plywood and raw and painted metal, were chosen to empathise with the original industrial shell. The working area is necessarily more restrained but sliding glass partitions/doors to private offices ensure an informal relationship between managers on the perimeter and workers in the centre. The most assertive object is the perforated metal clad structure, enclosing a small meeting space and printer room that sits below the roof junction of the two bays. Other gestures are comparatively more modest. The conventional and four square perimeter spaces are embellished by diverse patterns that ignore the demarcation of horizontal and vertical planes and present to the central space, through their transparent partitions, a parade of graphic set pieces that encourage interaction between managers and managed.

The project is distinguished as much for the wit and profligacy of its detail as it is for the impact of its, very, three dimensional set pieces. The iconoclasm that decorates the floor, walls and ceiling of the lavatories (labelled 'Holy Shit') with mosaic images, in the style of ecclesiastic frescoes that illustrate ironically company aspirations (labelled 'the Holy Shit List') encapsulates brand values with careless panache.

TOP
Immediately inside the very conventional entrance doors the obsessive distortion of vertical and horizontal begins.

BOTTOM
Along the length of the first bay facetted black planes wrap around and over meeting areas, with varying degrees of enclosure.

TOP
The angularity of the stair to the mezzanine is amplified by the interaction of the treads and the balustrade wall on the right.

BOTTOM LEFT
(Upper) 'Skin' (plywood and metal sheet)
(Lower) 'Bone's (steel structure)

BOTTOM RIGHT
The triangular window frames to the lower rooms are themselves angled. The existing roof trusses contribute their own triangularity.

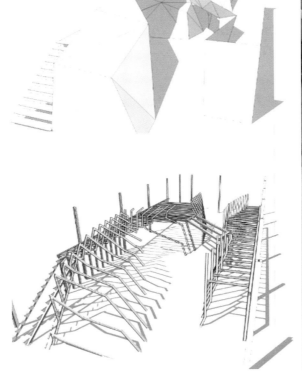

ABOVE LEFT & RIGHT
A void gives views up to the mezzanine and back down to the 'Hive', a layering of triangular shapes to which the light fittings contribute.

LEFT
Painted decoration in the Quiet Room in the first bay ignores the junctions of the facetted planes to add a less geometric element.

BOTTOM
The boardroom may be washed with a palette of coloured lighting, by day as well as night.

OPPOSITE
Plan
1 'The Landing' (entrance, reception and stair to mezzanine)
2 'The Dive' (social, meeting area with kitchen)
3 Boardroom
4 'Crash Room'
5 Bar
6 'Sound Clash'
7 Storage
8 Quiet room
9 'Holy Shit' (lavatories)
10 Marketing
11 'Mobile Timeout' (meeting room
12 Print room
13 Office

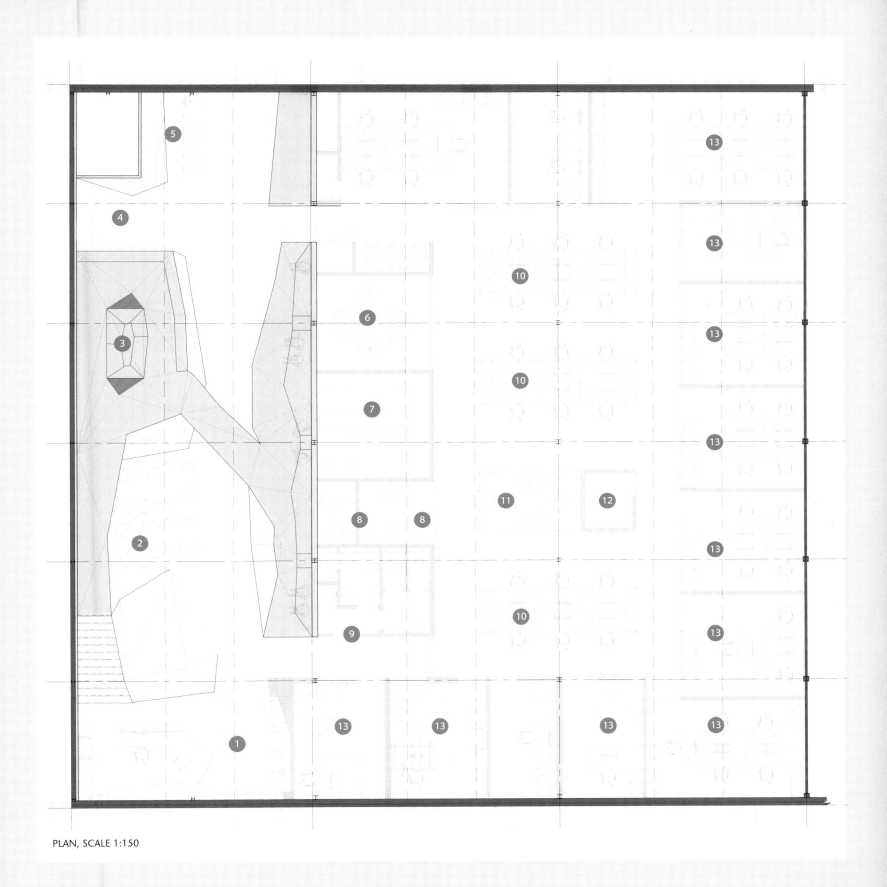

PLAN, SCALE 1:150

TOP LEFT
The unit, labelled 'Stratos', containing meeting place and print room in the work space is, geometrically restrained. Sloping planes respond directly to the valley between bays two and three.

TOP RIGHT
The aluminium framed glazing provides structure and acoustic privacy in the meeting room. The perforated metal cladding screen, mounted externally on the side walls provides visual privacy. The scale of pattern matches that in the perimeter offices.

BOTTOM LEFT
The plywood seating in the 'Quiet Room' doubles as storage.

BOTTOM RIGHT
Painted patterns spill off the wall and over the steps.

OPPOSITE TOP LEFT
Each small office has its own decorative motif. While walls, floors and ceilings meet at right angles patterns that slide between horizontals and verticals continue the assault on the right angle.

OPPOSITE TOP RIGHT
The 'op art' pattern launches the most dramatic deconstruction of the box.

OPPOSITE MIDDLE
Straight lines and blocks of colour, particularly when teamed with the subdivided floor, set up a perspectival diagram that again erodes conventional rectangularity.

OPPOSITE BOTTOM LEFT
Two and three dimensions work together in this reference to the company's sponsorship of airplane racing.

OPPOSITE BOTTOM RIGHT
The lavatories (labelled 'Holy Shit') are decorated with a mosaic that illustrates company activities and aspirations in parodies of ecclesiastic fresco imagery.

THIN OFFICE, SINGAPORE
STUDIO SKLIM

The designers point out that, while a laptop in a café may be an increasingly favoured method and place of 'work' (their inverted commas) it is still essential to have a permanent work (no inverted commas) environment but they also suggest that, within this traditional perception, there is now a need for flexibility, in response to less prescribed work patterns. The brief for this project required the new interior to accommodate two companies, one involved with IT and the other a multi-media setup added to the need for flexibility.

The shell, within a post war building in Singapore's central business district, offered a long and narrow split level volume and the designers chose to leave walls, ceilings and light fittings as found. The floor area was divided into eight territories, an informal reception, a long work top, a meeting table, semi-enclosed 'Boss Boxes' and, at the lower level, a slightly elevated meeting place, a multi-media area and a small kitchen. The lavatory and storage provision were the only wholly enclosed rooms. The organisation allowed hot desking, informal and spontaneous working clusters, and the 'Boss Boxes' offered retreats from the distractions of communal activity. The long work top, with its integrated strip of data and power points that allowed connections to be made anywhere along its length, accommodates up to ten workers. Its unbroken length transmutes into seating at the reception point and, at the lower level, the kitchen worktop and storage. The reductive logic of the detailing is typified by the two circular pads that cushion the bench at reception. The two 'Boss Boxes' and the raised 'Twist Platform' meeting place on the lower level might be accused of deviating from the general restraint.

The 'Boxes', one of them double sided, sit on an angled base that implies minimal contact with the floor. A few back panels omitted in the interlocking vertical and horizontal lengths of painted MDF, which separate both sides of the double unit provide the rigid composite structure and double as storage compartments, emphasise the commitment to shared space, even where the intention is to increase privacy.

The stepped entrance to the 'Twist Platform' suggests greater isolation than it provides. Its raised floor, counter intuitively, brings it close to the upper level but its walls stop short of the ceiling to allow its occupants a glimpse of the greater space beyond. The 'twisted' wall marks the intersection of the formal territories of the two businesses and enhances the small kitchen area and, in the section where the top twists back, becomes an inclined plane against users may lean.

PLAN, SCALE 1:150

OPPOSITE TOP
The exterior: a shabby building on a busy street.

OPPOSITE BOTTOM
Plan
1 Stair
2 Lift
3 Entrance
4 'Welcome Mat' (reception)
5 Long work top
6 Discussion table
7 'Boss Boxes' (semi private work stations)
8 'Recharging Point' (small kitchen)
9 'Twist Platform' (meeting space)
10 Multi-media area
11 Lavatory
12 Storage

RIGHT
The entrance area: A seat, with two cushions, occupies the upper level and abuts the small kitchen below. A slot in the high-level kitchen cupboard holds magazines.

BOTTOM
The long wall bench runs the length of the upper level. A continuous power track accommodates fluctuating numbers of users.

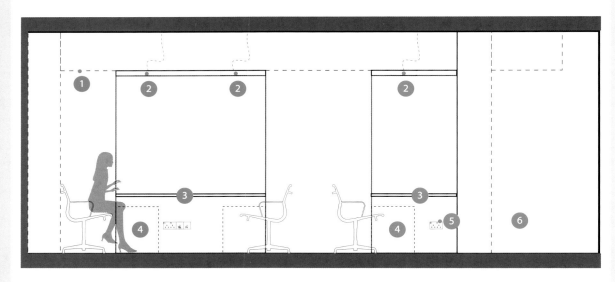

'BOSS BOXES', ELEVATION, SCALE 1:40

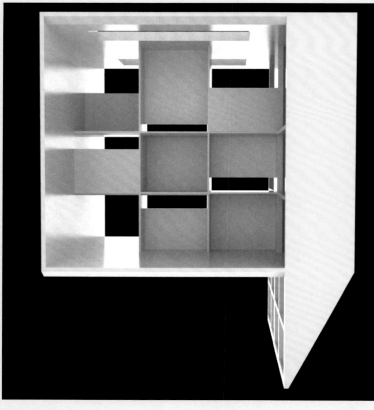

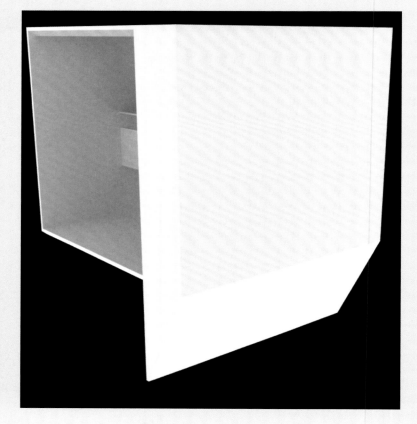

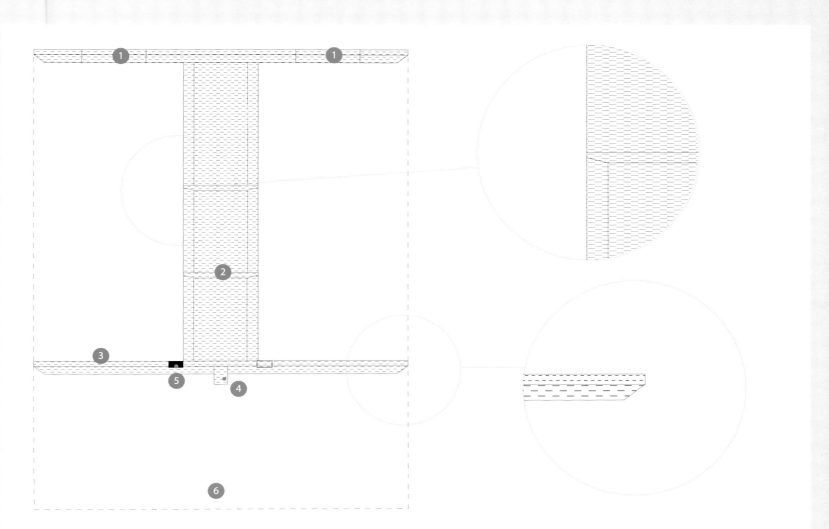

SECTION, SCALE 1:15

ABOVE
Section
1 Fluorescent light fitting set into 'roof'
2 Painted MDF shelf
3 Work top
4 Central support
5 Recessed power track
6 Floor level

RIGHT
The monolithic exterior of the boxes conceals the delicate grid of storage compartments.

LEFT
White steps lead to the lower area and black steps, which match the lighting structure over the 'Platform' meeting space. The 'twisted' wall is visible on the right.

BOTTOM
1 Existing structure
2 New walls
3 Fixed table with central slot for integral power source
4 Lower 'twisted' wall
5 Storage
6 Worktop – multimedia area
7 Platform floor level
8 'Twisted' wall
9 Lighting fixture

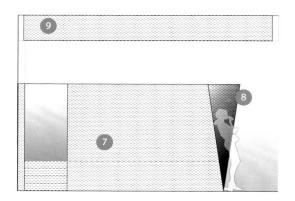

ELEVATION TO UPPER LEVEL, SCALE 1:75

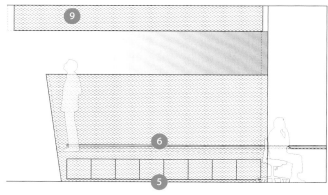

ELEVATION TO MULTI-MEDIA AREA, SCALE 1:75

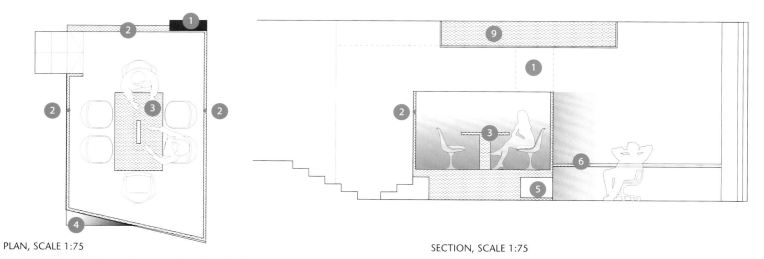

PLAN, SCALE 1:75

SECTION, SCALE 1:75

TOP LEFT
The 'twisted' wall leading to the multimedia area.

TOP RIGHT
The 'twisted' wall looking towards the upper level.

RIGHT
Diagram: 'twisted' wall configuration.

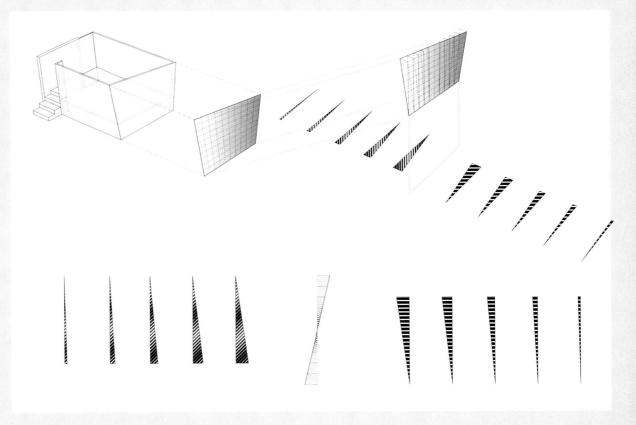

WOW, SENDAI
UPSETTERS ARCHITECTS

Perhaps it is because the visual language of the office building with its stacked floors of low, ribbon-windowed work rooms and its palette of suspended ceilings and demountable partitions has begun to achieve a degree of retro chic that designers are increasingly inclined to use its clichés as contextual foils.

WOW is an established visual design company, based in Tokyo, Sendai and Florence, and this refurbishment of its Sendai studio responds knowingly to a typically long, window-hugging space with panoramic views over the city. The floor area is generous for the number of staff, and this has allowed the designers to populate the space sparsely. Work places do not cling to the perimeter and there are no private offices to disrupt the volume. The only concession to privacy is a glass wall that separates the meeting room from the ongoing business of the studio and also connects the strip windows on both end elevations, which further emphasises the restraint of the new intervention.

At first sight only the pairing of desks establishes the beginnings of an organisational structure. What appears to be the crude minimalism, shared with every existing office shell, is exposed to scrutiny, but closer consideration reveals that the expediencies that characterise the normal shell are scrupulously eliminated here. What would normally be a gridded suspended ceiling of composite tiles is a plane of new, unpainted, plaster, broken only by the lines of light fittings and air conditioning slots that make a rationale for the location of the desks and stretch through the glass wall that encloses the meeting room. The wall and its door have none of the modular framing of the standard office partitioning system, the glass passing framelessly into floor and ceiling. Everything teeters on the brink of the mundane but that balancing act, between the everyday and the extraordinary, insinuates itself, however subliminally, into an observer's imagination. Furniture offers the most obvious hint that all is the result of creative deliberation. The framing of the desks indicates a well-informed eye and the sofa and table in the entrance area suggest quirky irony. The well-ordered shelving/partition between meeting room and storage room demonstrate an aesthetic pragmatism. But it is the incongruous stacking of raw wooden blocks beneath the long window, blatantly at odds with the mechanistic components of the normal office interior, that most clearly suggests a subversive intent. The invitation to staff to rearrange them, to make seats and tables, is a reassurance that they are involved in creative, collaborative initiatives.

TOP
Furniture in the entrance area offers an idiosyncratic take on the familiar components of an office reception area. The wooden blocks beneath the window suggest something radical.

MIDDLE
The apparently casual dispersal of desks and the unpainted plaster ceiling initially suggest the interior is unfinished. Even the entrance screen with its scant information suggests an interim expedient.

BOTTOM
The organic order of the wooden blocks contrasts with the machined precision of the desks and the clutter of wiring beneath them.

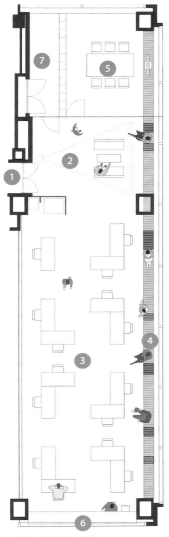

PLAN, SCALE 1:200

ABOVE
Plan
1 Entrance
2 Meeting area
3 Work space
4 Wooden blocks
5 Meeting room
6 Storage wall
7 Storage room

TOP RIGHT
The frameless glass wall between reception and meeting room allows the view to wrap around three sides. The edge of the shelving and the full height door beside it conform to the same reductive aesthetic. The meeting room furniture quietly refers to pieces that belong to the heyday of the multi-storey office block.

RIGHT
Hard edged restraint also prompts the squared configuration of the storage wall and its ordered cornice of files.

OFFICE 04, i29
AMSTERDAM

The client is an international digital marketing agency. The designers had to provide eighty workplaces for its Amsterdam office and establish a local identity that demonstrated a radical wit underpinned by serious intent and professional efficiency. They proposed a flexible place that would accommodate changing team structures, and would encourage and support creative interaction, a place of intimate work spaces for teams and individuals relieved by generous circulation routes.

Elements of the existing building shell could not be removed and prompted some of the fundamental decisions made about the new design. The designers' instinct was to unite old and new with a single grand gesture and they chose to achieve this with a defining finishing material, one that, in the first instance would offer a radical alternative to the conventional grid of acoustic ceiling tiles but would also perform as a cladding for the immovable elements and the remaining evidence of those removed. Acoustic control, crucial in the open work environment, suggested the use of a textile and further consideration identified felt as the most appropriate choice, one that was comparatively easy to apply across the new and existing surfaces. Felt's matt textured surface gave a uniform substance to all it clad. Its acoustic performance was particularly strong and it was easily fireproofed. It was durable, environmentally friendly, covered both hard substrates and soft furnishings, and gave visual unity to the whole.

In the finished interior the felt ceiling acts as a unifying element and the material continues down the faces and edges of the panels that enclose and define team work places. It is turned through ninety degrees again to become the desktop finish but is fragmented by the grey metal inserts that mark laptop positions, and its fragmentation integrates it with the hard, white glossy finishes of the desk components and chairs that in turn relate to the white plastic laminate flooring. The white tables that line the ribbon of windows are punctuated by felt-clad and cushioned seating 'boxes' that can accommodate one person seeking privacy or two in conversation. Felt cladding also makes very clear the intended connection between new semi-circular bench seats and the drum of the existing stair and lift shaft and the felting of light fittings, and the cables that feed them, leave no doubt about the project's conceptual intention.

TOP
Felted surfaces provide the visual identity and offer an environmentally friendly solution to acoustic performance and fire-proofing. Everything, including cables to light fittings, is transformed and unified.

BOTTOM
Circular elements relate to the existing vertical circulation core and to the felt screens that define work places.

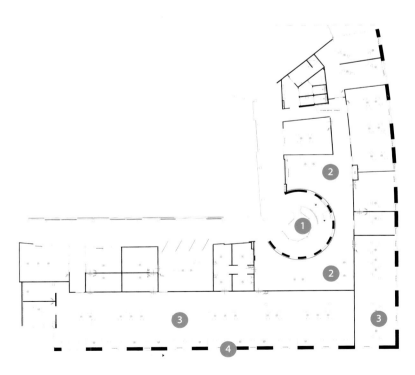

PLAN, SCALE 1:400

TOP

Felted screens touch the felted ceiling and close the ends of semi-private spaces for four or six workers. Enclosed seating boxes punctuate the work surface that runs beneath the window.

LEFT

Plan

1 Existing stair and lift enclosure

2 New felted seating units

3 Communal work tables

4 Seating 'boxes'

ABOVE

The felt of the screens is turned through ninety degrees to cover areas of the work surface. The seating boxes, felt lined with felt covered cushions, are located against solid areas of the external wall.

BBH,
LONDON
URBAN SALON

The advertising agency clients occupy the second, third and fourth floors, arranged around a large marble-clad atrium, of a speculative office block. The premises were upgraded in 2003 to reflect the company's departmental structure but the isolation of specialist divisions reduced opportunities for staff to work collaboratively and to share ideas. The clients wanted to change from a business with a creative department to one with creativity as their core activity. They wanted fluidity and a workplace that allowed staff to work in a variety of ways, in big or small groups, with external partners and freelancers. They preferred to upgrade their existing premises again, to retain their central London location.

Large tables, with their integrated sofas, at the bottom of the three storey atrium became the physical and symbolic heart of the organisation, a studio space that encourages creative and social interaction. They provide ad hoc meeting places and collaborative tools but may be moved to accommodate temporary events and company forum meetings, which may involve up to four hundred participants. Horizontal surfaces incorporated into the balustrades on the upper floors allow individuals to work while looking into, and connecting with the core space. Eleven 'think box' meeting rooms, with strongly coloured seating and patterned interiors, are distributed across the three floor levels, to provide havens for individuals and small group activities and, should it be necessary, retreats from the expanses of the communal work places. Work may be pinned up on their external and internal walls. Individual offices are ranged on the exterior walls on each floor.

The three floors are accessed from the street by a lift, clad in bamboo panels that anticipate the extensive use of the material in new elements throughout the interior. Visitors are carried directly to the third floor so that the organisation and its component parts stretches below and above them. The long straight bamboo clad front of the reception desk is angled to filter them towards the spectacle of the atrium. Internally the levels are connected by two straight, diagonally opposed, lengths of stairs grouped at one end of the atrium. The balustrades of one are clad in bamboo slats and those of the other in acoustic plasterboard with patterns of random dots. The two materials are continued in the horizontal balustrades around the atrium. A bamboo clad spiral stair connects the levels at the opposite end of the atrium. Acoustic control is augmented by timber clad fins that hang beneath the existing barrel-vaulted roof light and also provide solar shading.

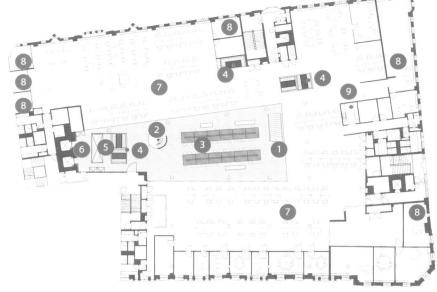

SECOND FLOOR PLAN, SCALE 1:500

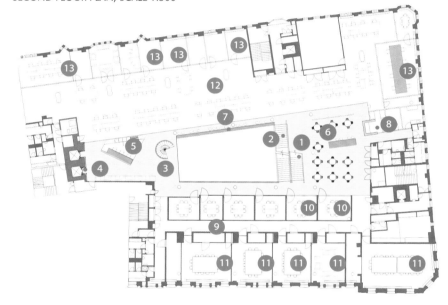

THIRD FLOOR PLAN, SCALE 1:500

FOURTH FLOOR PLAN, SCALE 1:500

OPPOSITE TOP

Second Floor Plan

1 Stair with acoustic plasterboard balustrade cladding

2 Spiral stair with bamboo balustrade cladding

3 Studio with movable furniture and integrated sofas

4 'Think Box' informal meeting room

5 Bicycle store

6 Lift lobby

7 Open plan office

8 Private office

9 Tea point

OPPOSITE MIDDLE

Third Floor Plan

1 Stair with acoustic plasterboard balustrade cladding

2 Stair with bamboo balustrade cladding

3 Spiral stair with bamboo balustrade cladding

4 Main lift lobby

5 Reception

6 Communal café

7 Balustrade shelf with high stools

8 Servery

9 Corridor gallery

10 Large meeting room

11 Meeting room

12 Open plan office

13 Private office

OPPOSITE BOTTOM

Fourth Floor Plan

1 Stair with acoustic plasterboard balustrade cladding

2 Stair with bamboo balustrade cladding

3 Spiral stair with bamboo balustrade cladding

4 'Think Box' informal meeting area

5 Lift lobby

6 Balustrade shelf with high stools

7 Meeting room

8 Open plan office

9 Tea point

10 Private office

RIGHT

The different acoustic claddings create interaction between stairs and balustrades. Acoustic fins also filter natural light from the original rooflight above.

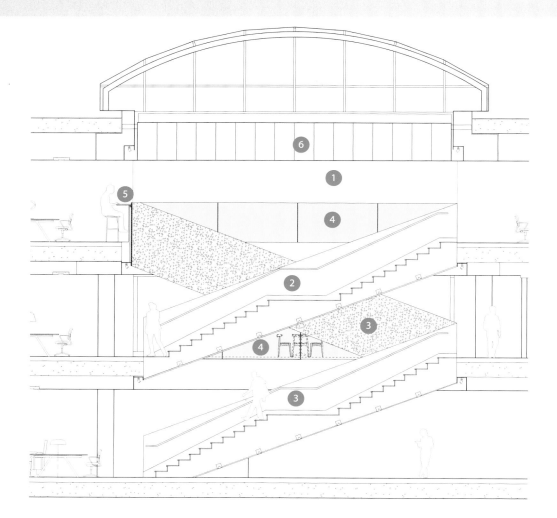

SECTION, SCALE 1:200

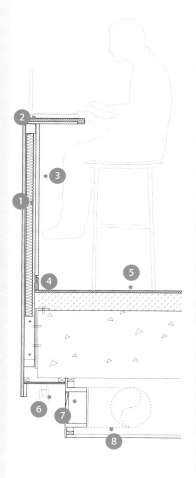

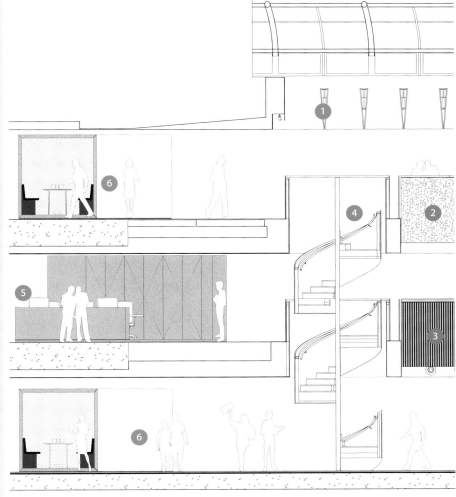

SECTION, SCALE 1:100

TOP LEFT
The bamboo clad spiral provides an alternative to the atrium stairs.

TOP RIGHT
Section through spiral stair
1 Acoustic fins
2 Acoustic plasterboard balustrade
3 Bamboo slat balustrade
4 Spiral stair with bamboo slat cladding
5 Reception desk with full height storage
6 'Think Box' meeting room

BOTTOM RIGHT
1 Glass to timber
2 Glass to timber with bar top
3 Stair handrail to timber balustrade
4 Stair handrail to timber balustrade with bar shelf
5 Stair handrail to glass balustrade to stair handrail
6 Stair handrail to glass balustrade

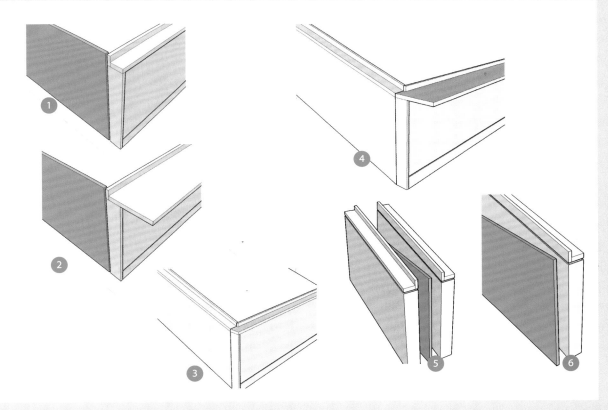

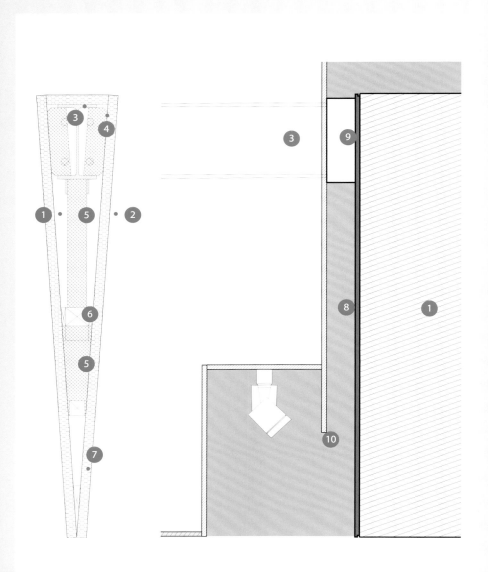

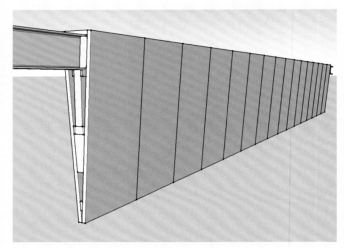

DETAIL, SCALE 1:10   DETAIL, SCALE 1:10

ABOVE LEFT AND RIGHT

ABOVE LEFT AND RIGHT
Acoustic Fin – Side Elevation – Junction
With Atrium Bulkhead
1 Woodwool acoustic panel painted
white
2 Woodwool acoustic panel painted blue
3 Steel beam
4 Timber infill piece
5 Timber rib
6 Mid height timber spar and packing
7 Bottom spar
8 Black stained MDF capping panel
9 White plasterboard cladding to steel
beam
10 Atrium bulkhead concealing spotlight

BOTTOM LEFT
Workers on stools sit individually or in
clusters along the high work tables on the
floor of the atrium. Upholstered seating
cut into the length of the table is served
by low tables and standard height chairs.

BOTTOM RIGHT
Random dots in the acoustic plasterboard
on one stair contrasts with the regularity
of bamboo slats on the other.

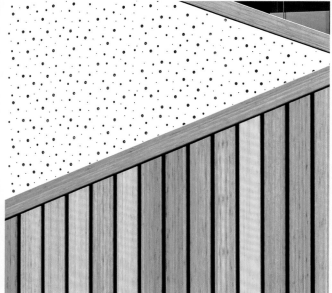

ABOVE
'Think Boxes' offer places of retreat from the expanses of shared work places and the volume of the atrium. Internal lighting glows through the 'Think Box' wall details.

RIGHT
Plan
1 Work table – linoleum top on solid bamboo panel
2 Removable upholstered seat
3 Bamboo clad frame
4 Bamboo clad exterior pin up walls

Elevation
1 Work table – linoleum top on solid bamboo panel
2 Removable upholstered seat
3 Dark grey laminate
4 Access panel for sprinkler maintenance
5 Wall mounted light fitting
6 Picture frame and artwork on pin up board
7 Wallpaper

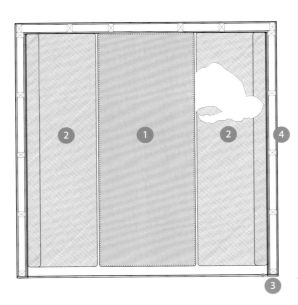

PLAN, SCALE 1:35

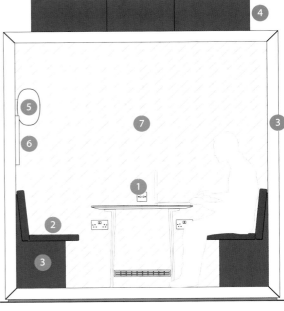

ELEVATION, SCALE 1:35

HEADVERTISING, BUCHAREST
CORVIN CRISTIAN

These offices for an advertising agency occupy part of the shell of the former Rumanian stock exchange. The brief asked for an interior that could respond to sudden, often short term, changes in the physical organisation of the company and, while it had to consolidate an impression of efficiency, it also had to appeal to the creative, predominantly young, employees. The designers built their solution on what they perceived to be a commitment, shared by the former and present occupants of the building to moving commodities in the pursuit and promotion of commerce and that idea of movement gelled neatly with the practicalities of a flexible interior.

The essential components in the resolution of concept and function are storage cabinets, which sit on generously sized castors and may be moved to subdivide and reconfigure working areas. The lower of the two cabinet types match the height of the screens that typically divide work stations and the higher, while stopping short of the ceiling, provide visual privacy but with a more impressive presence than a conventional demountable full-height partition. The matt grain of naturally finished plywood used for cabinet shells and shelves sits well with the textures and flat greys of the exposed concrete walls of the original building.

The tall cabinets flank the glass walls and provide partial visual privacy to the meeting room which is the most pristine element in the new interior. Its butt jointed clear glass panels separate its plywood floor from its plywood ceiling and these horizontal planes are themselves visually separated from the existing floor and ceiling so that the unit appears to hover and gives the impression that a gentle push might propel it across the empty expanse of floor.

While the refinement of the meeting room and the well crafted cabinets do suggest organisational efficiency, the agency's lighter side is demonstrated by the interlocking plywood pedestals of the oversized table lights that sit on low cabinets. These, like the cabinets, were made in small local workshops. Well padded leather sofas complete the nods to tradition and occasional kitsch ornaments invite employees to make their own contributions to softening any impression of a corporate aesthetic. The agency itself does choose to present a relaxed face to clients who enter through a generously scaled staff recreation room which is dominated by a table tennis table and the brightly coloured hand and foot grips of an improvised climbing wall. The vinyl letters that spell the company name on the two glass walls confirm that the serious creative work happens beyond.

OPPOSITE TOP

The meeting room appears to float above the original floor level and below the ceiling, suggesting that, like the new storage pieces, it may be moved. Plywood finishes to floor and ceiling match the new furniture.

OPPOSITE BOTTOM

The new cabinets define desk layouts. Their wheels declare them to be transient but the raw textures of their plywood panelling relate convincingly to those of the existing wall surfaces.

RIGHT

Plywood is also used for the over-sized table lamps that mimic, with interlocking two-dimensional profiles, the shafts of more modestly scaled traditional fittings. A toy aeroplane confirms the commitment to wood.

BOTTOM

Plan
1 Entrance
2 Stair
3 Lift
4 Table tennis table
5 Climbing wall
6 Production department
7 Client service department
8 Meeting room
9 Creative department
10 Kitchen
11 Balcony
12 Lavatories

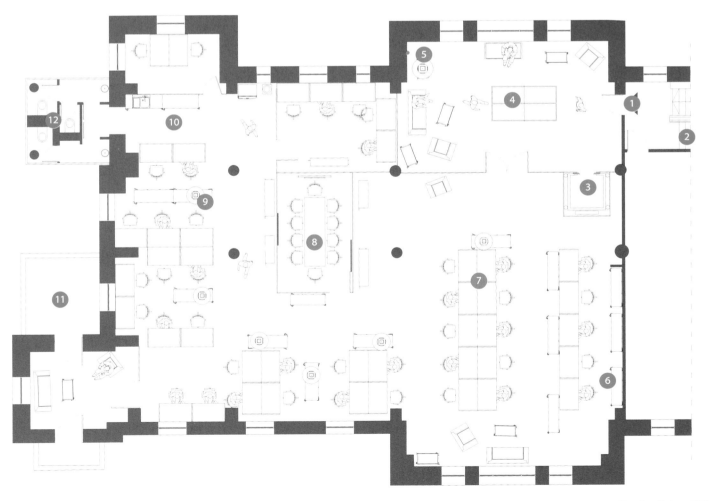

PLAN, SCALE 1:150

OPPOSITE TOP

A ceramic ornament is one of the idiosyncrasies that undermine any impression of a conventional office fit out

OPPOSITE BOTTOM LEFT

Vinyl lettering spelling the company name wraps around the two glass walls of the arrival and relaxation room.

OPPOSITE BOTTOM RIGHT

The rawness of the plywood cabinets echoes the texture of the walls.

RIGHT

Traditional leather sofas and armchairs sit comfortably against raw concrete and brick.

BOTTOM LEFT

The lettering creates an acceptable degree of visual separation the relaxation room and the office proper.

BOTTOM RIGHT

The principles of storage and mobility also define a low table.

PRIDE AND GLORY INTERACTIVE, KRAKOW
MORPHO STUDIO

The client is a design-led advertising agency that wanted an interior that was both an efficient and inspiring workplace and which gave it a clear identity. The site is an old cable factory in Krakow's industrial district and the designer's decision was to preserve what she calls the 'sentimental atmosphere' found in any abandoned workplace but to 'warm up' the new environment while accommodating the trappings of a modern office and meeting the priorities of a less noisy, less physical activity.

The subdivision of the empty shell is prompted in part by the location of existing columns. Up to seventy employees are accommodated in groups of no more than eight, in spaces small enough to be intimate but not wholly enclosed, with at least one side open to circulation zones. Sometimes walls, sometimes storage shelving and sometimes free-standing columns mark the boundaries of dedicated spaces. The utilitarian elements of the existing building fabric are painted a uniform white but remain as found. The black surface mounted electrical cable and conduit reflect the same direct approach and, with the black shades on the various new suspended light fittings, make a connection between the existing elements and the new, predominantly black, chairs and computer equipment that necessarily litter the new rooms. The enthusiasm for exposed cabling is confirmed by the aggregation of looped cables that sketch the outlines of a chandelier in the smaller meeting room and the sweeping black lines of Starck's Masters chairs, used around the kitchen table. Many of the detailing decisions display a wit that is not immediately obvious but its presence is signalled clearly and early in the cardboard stag's head decorations that hang on the wall of the first meeting space immediately behind reception.

Timber finishes sit between the extremes of black and white and bring warmth and tonal variation. Timbers reclaimed from the house of one of the clients and used for shelving, reception desk and some tables, bring one hundred years of patination to the mix. While new timber is used, with a diagrammatic simplicity, in bespoke furniture pieces its most assertive application is in the heavy doors to meeting rooms that stand isolated in glass walls on either side and above them. While apparently traditionally detailed the doors necessarily depends for stability on a concealed steel frame fixed to the floor and given some additional support from the 8mm (⅜ in) glazing panels.

RIGHT
Reclaimed timber panels, stacked with reclaimed timber spacers make the reception desk. Less glamorously, three stacked timber pallets make a low table.

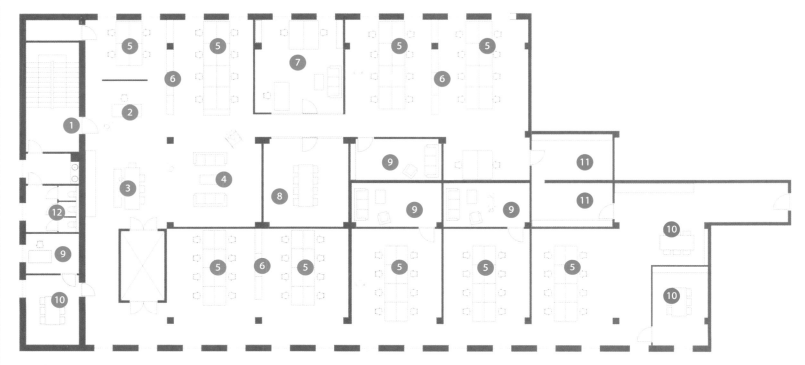

PLAN, SCALE 1:200

TOP
Plan
1 Entrance
2 Reception
3 Kitchen
4 Waiting/relaxation area
5 Shared office space
6 Storage wall
7 Communal office (with glazed wall)
8 Meeting room (with glazed wall)
9 Private office/meeting room
10 Meeting places
11 Storage
12 Lavatory

LEFT
New furniture, fixtures and fittings are predominantly black and linked by the black electrical cabling fixed casually to the white painted original building fabric.

OPPOSITE TOP
The elemental wooden blocks of the kitchen table, bench and stool match the solidity of the reclaimed timber. Black table legs link timber to the plastic of the Masters chairs.

OPPOSITE BOTTOM LEFT
The twisting black lines of Starck's Masters chair echo the cabling. The triangular form of the black rubber light fitting has an affinity with the angled support of the display shelves.

OPPOSITE BOTTOM RIGHT
Cardboard stag's head wall decorations signal the wit that elevates what may appear to be simple detailing.

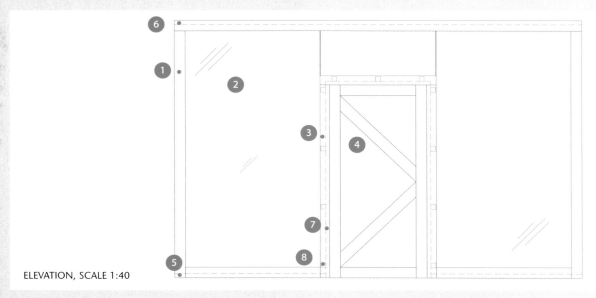

ELEVATION, SCALE 1:40

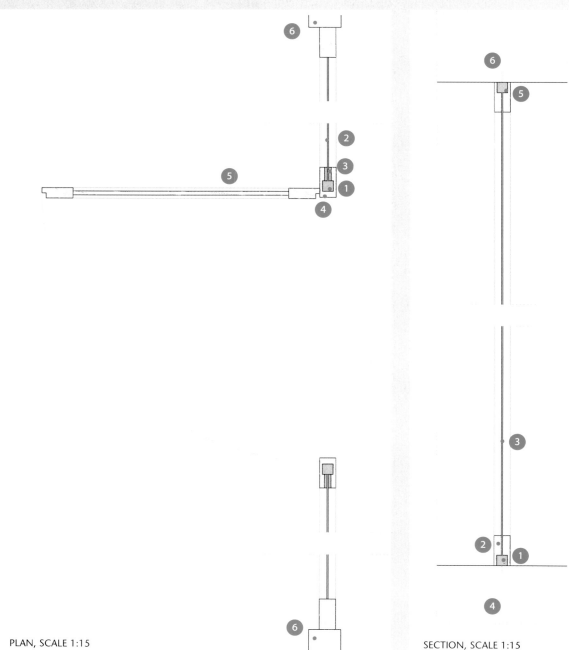

PLAN, SCALE 1:15

SECTION, SCALE 1:15

LEFT
Elevation of timber door
1 115x40mm (4½ x 1½ in) timber window frame
2 8mm (⅜ in) glass
3 Timber cladding frame to steel structural frame
4 Solid timber door leaf
5 Steel channel frame fixed to concrete floor
6 Steel head channel fixed to concrete beam
7 Steel door frame
8 52x52mm (2x2 in) hollow steel frame

BOTTOM LEFT
Timber door plan detail
1 52x52mm (2x2 in) hollow steel frame
2 8mm (⅜ in) glass
3 53x15mm (2 x ⅝ in) steel door frame
4 Timber cladding to conceal steel frame
5 Solid timber door leaf
6 Masonry wall

BOTTOM RIGHT
Glazed wall section detail
1 Steel frame fixed to concrete beam
2 Timber cladding to conceal steel frame
3 8mm (⅜ in) glass
4 Concrete floor
5 Steel frame fixed to concrete beam
6 Concrete ceiling structure

OPPOSITE TOP
The solid timber door stands, seemingly independently, in the timber framed glazed wall. The black surface-mounted electrical conduit and cabling evolve to become an embryonic chandelier, its form traced by the looped and hanging cables.

OPPOSITE BOTTOM LEFT
Timber cladding pieces hide the structural steel frame that supports the solid timber door leaf.

OPPOSITE BOTTOM RIGHT
In contrast to the heavy, ostensibly traditional, detailing of the door leaf the timber Troag light fittings introduce curves and colour stains.

SIERRA SPACE, SAN FRANCISCO
LOJO I

The Sierra Club, founded in 1892 to encourage appreciation of, and as a lobbying group to campaign for, the protection of the Sierra Nevada Mountains, is now the oldest and largest environmental organisation in the world. It is a non-profit making body with its income primarily directed into political campaigning and Sierra Space is its new reception area, created in 2011 to replace an unprepossessing original. Although the budget for the refurbishment was modest, the solution had to have visual impact, to present a more impressive public face to donors. The brief asked for the transformation of the space within a three month period and on a minimal budget. All materials used in the project are reclaimed, emit no, or low, rates of volatile organic compounds and are easily recyclable.

Once evidence of the original elements had been eliminated the airy but robust space seemed appropriate to the spirit of the organisation. For the essential additional element, the reception desk, the designers drew on images of logs piled in lumberyards and on the growths of ferns and mosses on fallen tree trunks, which symbolised for them the interdependence of elements within a continuing ecosystem. Stacked lengths of reclaimed Douglas Fir timber perform as the public face of the reception desk. For stability these are threaded over steel tubes, welded to square plates that are bolted to the existing concrete floor.

Recesses cut into the top edge of the top two logs accommodate rectangular stainless steel pans, which act as planters. These contain native Northern Californian oxygenating plants that contribute to air purification of the space. The length of timber that lies on the central long axis of the room and is already buried flush with the face of the existing concrete floor, connects the stacked logs to the original building fabric.

Ribbons of LED lights are concealed in recesses in the front edge of each log. The soft glow they emit contrasts with and accentuates the textures of the timber and contributes low ambient light to the space. A 3mm (⅛ in) aluminium sheet is folded to form the worktop of the desk and is dressed up the rear vertical and upper faces of the top log. A plywood spacer piece floats the flat, grey, thin and precise aluminium visually above the richly hued and textured timber. The desk sits in front of a pixellated image of the Yosemite Valley, one of the places that inspired the formation of the Club.

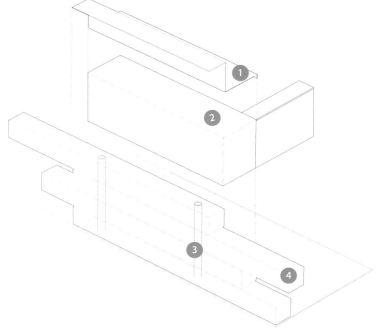

TOP
Squared lengths of Douglas Fir 'logs' are stacked to form the front of the reception desk. Their dimensions match that of the timber embedded in the concrete floor.

MIDDLE
The new timbers, staggered like logs stacked in a lumber yard, sit in front of a pixellated image of the Sierra Nevada Mountains on the wall behind.

BOTTOM
Exploded axonometric view
1 3mm (⅛ in) aluminium plate.
2 19mm (¾ in) birch plywood desk
3 50mm (2 in) diameter steel pipe
welded to 100mm (4 in) square plate bolted to existing floor
4 Sustainably sourced 300x300mm (4 x 4 in) Douglas Fir timber.

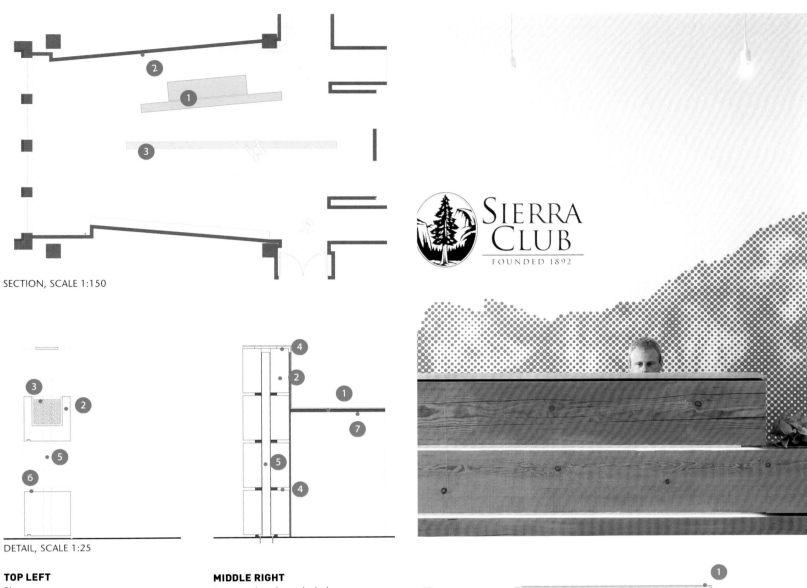

SECTION, SCALE 1:150

DETAIL, SCALE 1:25

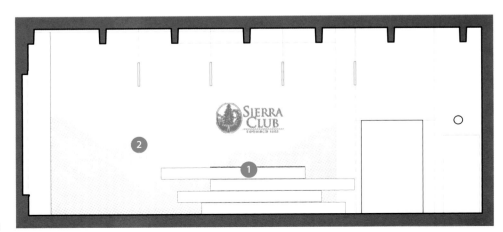

TOP LEFT

Plan

1 Desk

2 Vinyl mural on painted gypsum board

3 Existing timber beam embedded in the floor

TOP RIGHT

LED lights in the gaps between logs emphasise the timber's rough texture. The aluminium desk top 'floats' visually.

MIDDLE LEFT

Cross sections through desk

1 Mill-finished aluminium plate

2 Sustainably sourced Douglas Fir timber

3 Stainless steel planter set in routed slots

4 19mm (¾ in) plywood spaces screwed to timber

5 50mm (2 in) diameter steel pipe welded to 100mm (4 in) square plate bolted to existing floor

6 19mmx10mm (¾ x ⅜ in) routed groove for white LED ribbon strip light

7 19mm (¾ in) birch plywood desk carcase

MIDDLE RIGHT

Long section through desk

1 Mill-finished aluminium plate

2 Sustainably sourced Douglas Fir timber

3 Stainless steel planter

4 19mm (¾ in) plywood spaces screwed to timber

5 50mm (2 in) diameter steel pipe welded to 100mm (4 in) square plate bolted to existing floor

BOTTOM RIGHT

Section

1 Desk front

2 Vinyl mural

SECTION, SCALE 1:50

SECTION, SCALE 1:100

TVS, CHENNAI
MANCINI ENTERPRISES

This renovation of an existing office building for TVS, a company founded in 1911 and now principally operating in transportation and related financial sectors, involved the development of a ground floor lobby, four floors of corporate offices and a rooftop cafeteria. The entrance lobby introduces design themes and a materials palette that evolve on the upper floors. Strips of teak, the favoured timber, line the wide entrance portal and in the suspended lighting track teak veneers are contained by solid teak edge mouldings. Granite floor tiles mark the footprint of the track and the stone and clad the wall opposite the door that bears the company's name and logo.

Granite reappears quickly in the first floor reception area, in the three metre long table. Six granite panels, supported and elevated on three metal feet, make a substantial front for a teak table top and storage unit. A flat metal upright extends from each foot and projects back to support the metal frame that in turn carries the table top. Two gaps, equivalent to the width of the upright, separates the three pairs of slabs and a 50mm (2 in) gap separates the slabs and table top. The back corners of the table are supported on legs that are pairs of curved flats. The company's name is spelled out in substantial brass letters, recessed into the top of the slabs, and its logo is printed on one of the white blinds that mask the existing windows.

The other major furniture piece, in the principal meeting room, employs the material, and evolves the geometry, of the entrance lobby's light. A circular table, big enough to accommodate twelve comfortably, sits beneath a circular light fitting. A brass rail surrounds the empty centre of the table and a projector hangs in the empty centre of the light. The table's twelve cantilevered supporting legs meet the floor on the line of its inner edge and mark out the seating positions. The inner and outer edges of both table and light are generous mouldings of solid teak with lengths of teak veneer, on a plywood base that radiate from the centre between them.

The same device, of a table with a light fitting repeating its geometry and dimensions, is repeated in the secondary meeting room but a more modest rectangle replaces the circle and the paired, splayed leg components are a restrained version of those supporting the reception table. Throughout the building teak, in solid form and veneers, is used for grid patterns and panels on partitions, integrated shelving and storage furniture.

TOP
The teak strips that line the entrance portal represent the first application of the wood that forms the primary decorative element in the interior.

BOTTOM
Teak trim, sweeping curves and granite are further expressions of the decorative language.

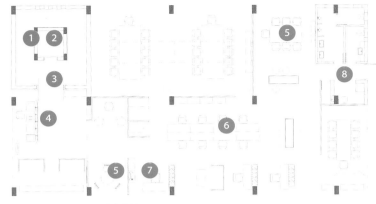

FIRST FLOOR PLAN, SCALE 1:300

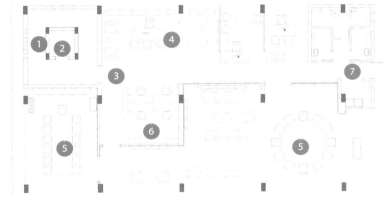

FOURTH FLOOR PLAN, SCALE 1:300

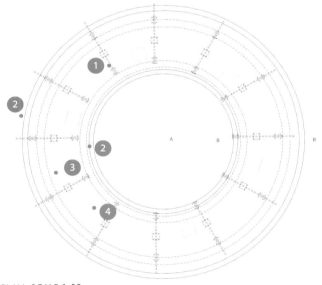

PLAN, SCALE 1:50

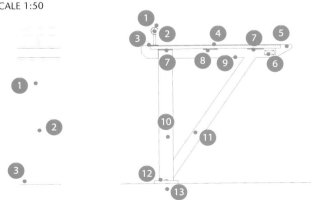

ELEVATION A, SCALE 1:20   SECTION B-B SCALE 1:20

TOP
First Floor Plan
1 Stair
2 Lift
3 Entrance
4 Reception
5 Conference and meeting rooms
6 Informal meeting and work place
7 Phone booths
8 Lavatories and kitchen

MIDDLE
Fourth Floor Plan
1 Stair
2 Lift
3 Entrance
4 Private offices
5 Board rooms
6 Secretaries
7 Lavatories and kitchen

BOTTOM
Plan: circular table
1 Mild steel frame and support below
2 Teak edging strip
3 Teak veneered plywood table top
4 Plywood box for power sockets under table top with press-open veneered lid
Elevation A
1 Mild steel flat
2 Mild steel flat spacer
3 Mild steel base plate
Section BB
1 Brass tube cut to profile
2 LED strip
3 Mild steel base plate
4 Teak veneer strips on plywood substrate
5 Teak edging machined to profile
6 Cut-out for cable tray
7 Curved mild steel flat
8 Mild steel flat
9 Mild steel spacer
10 Mild steel flat
11 Mild steel flat
12 Mild steel base plate
13 Anchor bolts

TOP RIGHT
In the principal meeting room the teak edged and veneered light fitting reflects the footprint of the table beneath it.

BOTTOM RIGHT
1 Anchor bolt fixings to existing floor soffit
2 High strength suspension cable
3 Mild steel T-section
4 Curved mild steel flat
5 Turn buckle
6 Light fitting
7 Teak edging strip machined to profile
8 Teak veneer on plywood
9 LED strip light
10 Brass tube cut to profile
11 Mild steel base plate

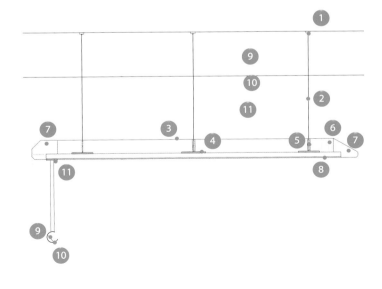

SECTION SCALE 1:20

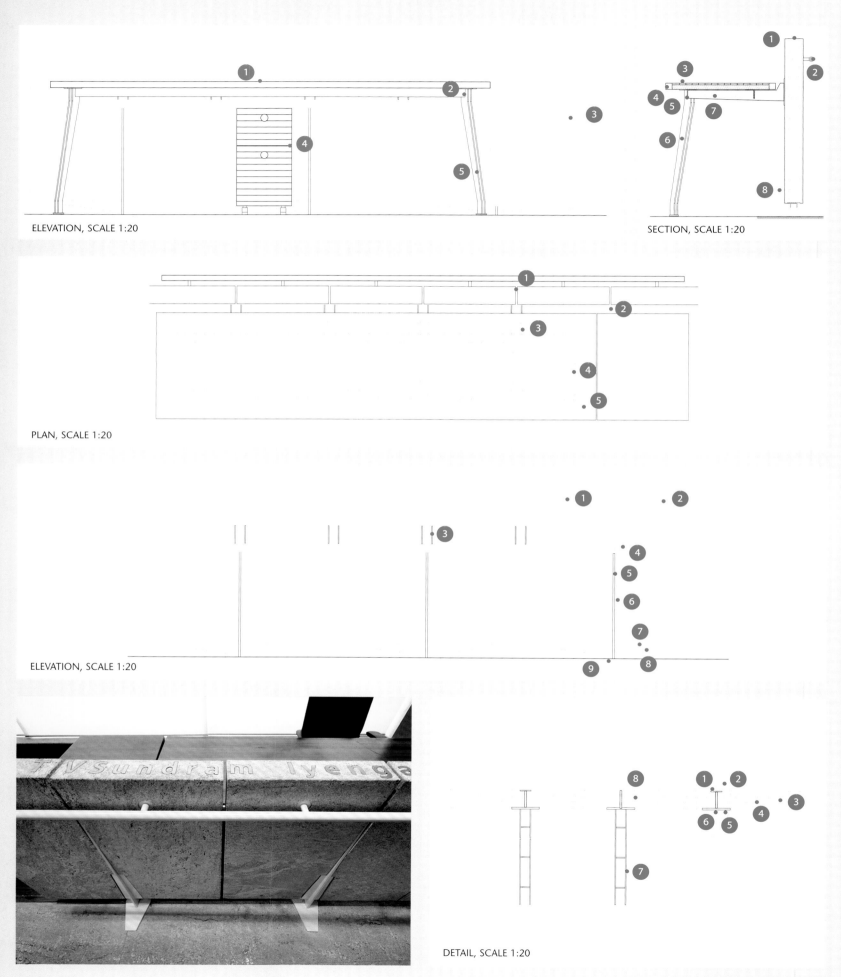

ELEVATION, SCALE 1:20

SECTION, SCALE 1:20

PLAN, SCALE 1:20

ELEVATION, SCALE 1:20

DETAIL, SCALE 1:20

OPPOSITE TOP LEFT

Rear elevation: reception desk
1 Electrical box
2 Mild steel section
3 Moveable storage unit
4 Moveable storage unit
5 Mild steel table legs

OPPOSITE TOP RIGHT

Section: reception desk
1 Hand dressed granite
2 Brass rail supported on long brass studs
3 Timber strip desk top
4 Solid timber edge strip
5 Mild steel T-section
6 Mild steel table leg
7 Mild steel support with three intermediate stiffeners
8 Mild steel powder-coated support for granite slabs

OPPOSITE MIDDLE

Plan: reception desk top support structure
1 Mild steel granite slab support – no floor contact
2 Mild steel granite and table top support – floor contact
3 Mild steel horizontal table top supports with intermediate stiffeners
4 White powder-coated mild steel section
5 White powder-coated mild steel leg

OPPOSITE LOWER MIDDLE

Rear elevation: reception desk, no table
1 5mm (⅕ in) groove in granite
2 Brass end cap over mounting for rail support
3 Mild steel horizontal table top supports with intermediate stiffeners
4 Mild steel plate recessed into granite
5 Mild steel vertical central support plate
6 Mild steel vertical support recessed into granite
7 Mild steel horizontal support plate recessed into granite
8 Mild steel support plate
9 Recess mounted base plate

OPPOSITE BOTTOM LEFT

Brass letters spelling the company name and that of its founder are set into the top edge of the granite. The finish of the handrail matches that of the feet.

OPPOSITE BOTTOM RIGHT

Plan: mild steel support structure
1 Vertical support plate
2 Base plate recessed into floor
3 Horizontal mild steel support plate
4 Vertical mild steel support plate
5 Support plate recessed into granite
6 Vertical mild steel central support plate
7 Mild steel horizontal table top supports with intermediate stiffeners
8 Position of granite slabs

TOP LEFT

On the first floor granite panels that front the teak work surface and cupboards of the reception desk run parallel to the

granite flooring strip from the stair and lift lobby.

TOP RIGHT

The granite slabs echo those on the wall of the lobby.

BOTTOM RIGHT

Exploded isometric
1 Desk top
2 Support frame for desk top
3 Rear corner leg
4 Support for table top and granite
5 Granite

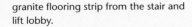
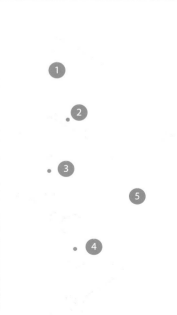

SOCIAL 01, DELFT

i29

Combiwerk is a training company created within the Delft region to prepare people who have varying degrees of handicap, whether physical, psychological or intellectual, for the workplace. It assesses individual needs, determines aptitudes and provides the focused training and support necessary for its clients to make a successful transition into full or part time jobs either within Combiwerk's own business service companies or with external employers.

The designers' task was to develop an area, surrounded by the workplaces, that would function as the company restaurant and a place for training and assessment. In contrast to the monochromatic strategy they chose to employ in their Office 04 project (pages 112-113) here they reacted against the grey exterior and the grey interior finishes that prevailed throughout the rest of the building and among them established islands of intense colour. The boundaries of these sanctuaries are defined by areas of coloured carpet and by stylised three-dimensional structures that carry the strong blues, greens, reds and yellows that counterpoint the light grey backdrops and suggest storage boxes. This is deliberate symbolism on the part of the designers, representing both the 'boxes' into which Combiwerk's clients are segregated and the many 'boxes' of opportunities that they can achieve. The massing of dividing structures creates natural areas for tonal variations within each of the islands. Tonal colour shifts are echoed in the subdivision of table surfaces and in the layouts of carpet tiles. The vertical and horizontal grid pattern of the boxes adds variations of light and shade.

The designers found out, in conversation with the interior's potential users, that most, to a greater or lesser degree, formed attachments to familiar surroundings and routines. While the emphatic nature of the coloured 'islands' ensured that they would quickly establish themselves as reassuring landmarks, the designers created a bridge for new users by assembling a collection of two hundred and fifty different second hand chairs that offered something that was modestly and reassuringly familiar. All were restored and finished in the same colour by one of the Combiwerk businesses and offered another opportunity for a symbolic gesture; each user can find the style of chair that suits them best but all chairs are united by the shared finish.

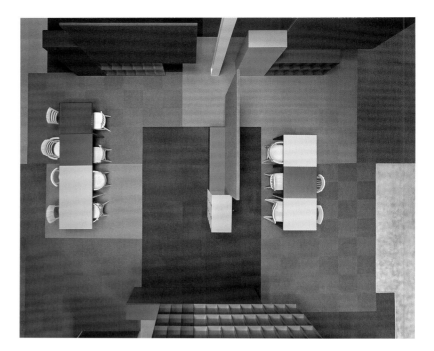

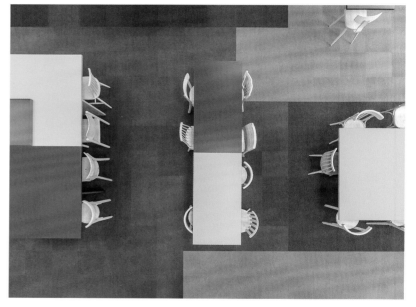

TOP & MIDDLE
Tonal variations further enrich the islands of colour and define territory at both floor and table top levels.

BOTTOM
The intense colours of the insertions clearly assert themselves against the greys of the existing shell.

TOP

The massing of the new elements rationalises the blocking in of tonal variation, which is amplified by shadows within the gridded structures.

ABOVE LEFT

The interaction and overlaying of the colours and tones of each of the islands makes a composition that is more than the sum of its parts.

ABOVE RIGHT

The very simple detailing of the new tables is a foil for more intricate forms of the reclaimed chairs, which are emphasised by being stripped of colour.

YMEDIA, WINK AND YPERFORM MADRID
STONE DESIGNS

Three related digital media companies share this twelve hundred square metre floor of a Madrid office block. While the activities of each were broadly similar there was a design imperative to ensure that identities and territories were demonstrated so that employees recognised their primary commitment while benefitting from the broader social interaction, and the symbiotic possibilities, that might be generated in the shared canteen

The designers wanted to give employees, individually and in groups, a place where they belonged, equivalent to 'home', with the whole floor, encompassing the territory of the other companies representing their 'neighbourhood'. No walls divided territories, which has advantages if areas are reassigned in the future, but the various aggregations of enclosed rooms give some structure to the plan. These enclosed areas are expressed as small separate 'buildings' and, even when arranged as a terrace, are detailed as distinct entities, by serrated elevations and fragments of sloping 'roofs'. They provide landmarks. Their responsibility for spatial demarcation is shared by the long worktables, which typically accommodate six or eight people, substantial objects to which individuals or project teams may attach themselves.

The material palette is shared across all areas. A single timber, oak, is favoured, whether in solid or veneer form and represents the designers' intention to introduce the reassurances of a natural world into the pragmatic aesthetic of the modern office block. It covers the floor in 200mm (8 in) wide boards, which also clad the lower sections of wall, so that the blurred distinction between wall and floor planes matches the porosity of territorial boundaries. Company territories are distinguished by the bright and strongly coloured fabrics that cover the low screens that divide workstations on the communal tables. These divisions slope gently along their length with adjacent pieces sloping in opposite directions. They suggest a landscape of hillocks, in which the 'buildings' sit. Ymedia colours are warm, red, yellow and ochre, perhaps accelerating the pace of work, the greens in Wink and the blues in Yperform are cooler, perhaps more likely to encourage reflection. Lengths of fabric in company colours and suspended from linear light fittings, supplementing the sense of company territory. Isolated spots of colour are scattered thinly across all areas, in the corner posts of oak cladding, light fittings and furniture, reminding employees of their commonality.

TOP
The degree of enclosure varies. The folded corner remains constant.

MIDDLE
Blocks of colour, areas of clear and translucent glass arranged on stepped plans identify individual meeting rooms

and offices. The folded external corner suggests a sloping roof.

BOTTOM
The principles of separate 'buildings' and blocks of colour are interpreted for the communal staff canteen.

TOP
The apparently random distribution of colour blocks and imagery against oak flooring and wall cladding anticipates the strategy throughout the interior.

BOTTOM
Plan
1 Stair

2 Lift lobby
3 Reception
4 Workstations (Ymedia)
5 Workstations (Wink)
6 Workstations (Yperform)
7 Meeting/work rooms
8 Private offices
9 Lavatories

GROUND FLOOR PLAN, SCALE 1:400

OPPOSITE TOP
The opposing slopes of longitudinal dividing screens suggest a 'landscape' in which the 'buildings' sit.

OPPOSITE BOTTOM
Spots of borrowed colour, in partition framing pieces, light fittings, graphics, bring a degree of commonality to the floor.

TOP
Fabric softens the line of, and light from, the fittings on which it hangs.

RIGHT
Each company has its own colour palette.

ANNVIL OFFICE, RIGA
ANNVIL

Designers' own offices are, for good or ill, a declaration of their values and capabilities. The stated premise underpinning this example is that colour affects how people react to their environments but a number of other principles, the use of text, the balancing of existing and new elements and the implications of temporary occupation, are equally significant and together generate a rewardingly complex statement.

Blocks of sharp colours, most often employed in the bought and bespoke furniture act as counterpoints to the white tones and pastel tints of walls and ceilings. Intended as stimuli for the creative imagination, the deliberation behind the strategy is signalled by their idiosyncratic deployment, on the tops of skirtings and the edges of furniture. They are convincing demonstrations of the potent impact of small intense passages of colour against large expanses of neutral ground. Their emphatic, perhaps discordant, presence is more likely to prompt creative action than the prescriptive experience of a room saturated with a single colour.

The location of texts, some aspirational, some provocative and some obscure follows the principle that perverse placement, low in a corner, high above a door, will signal serious intent. The English language piece, with its expletive knowingly obscured within a composite word, demonstrates the designer's confidence not only with the lingua franca of design but with the quality of her work. The single word 'tagad', which means 'now' in Latvian, painted messily in a questionable font above a traditional door frame, which has been messily stripped of its layers of paint, implies an impulse to reconsider the relationship of tradition and modernity in a particular geographical and social context. That the paint for the text has been allowed to drip over the frame suggests that the traditional will not be shown excessive respect. The presumption that these will not be the long term premises of the practice demonstrates ambition and the particular detailing of major pieces, such as the bespoke shelving unit, the mirror and the picture, that would normally be securely fixed in position, makes the expectation of moving on explicit. There is wit and irony in the recycled furniture and fittings that convincingly demonstrates a capacity to deal with expediencies.

TOP
Strong colours against white walls, eccentric objects, text oddly applied in odd places are the essence of the project's vocabulary.

such as the text in the left hand corner, additional potency. The repetitive quilting pattern of the sofa's upholstery has an affinity with the pattern of the parquet flooring.

MIDDLE
Existing doors and parquet floor provide readymade grandeur and give additions,

BOTTOM
This most provocative expression of studio values is tucked low in a corner.

ABOVE

The yellow edge to the mirror frame, the orange line on the skirting, which draws the eye from its imperfect junction with the floorboards, the stripped doors and the elegant lines of the bicycle are the more significant against the self-effacing white of floor, walls and ceiling.

TOP RIGHT

Characterful existing elements are balanced by the modern and the mundane, the painting leant casually against the wall, the miscellaneous utilitarian chairs, the tables. The light fitting, which belongs to a period between ancient and modern bridges the gap.

MIDDLE RIGHT

A more modest light fitting hangs beneath a more modest ceiling. The frame of the rocking chair is painted to match the skirting line. The shelving/cupboard structure that leans against the wall demonstrates an ambition to expand the business and move on as much as a respectful reluctance to interfere with existing elements.

BOTTOM RIGHT

'Tagad' means 'now' in Latvian. The drips of paint left on the crudely stripped door frame prompts thinking about how reverentially existing elements should be treated in the present.

HILL+KNOWLTON, RIGA
ANNVIL

This hostel occupies part of an old hemp factory in North East Italy. While subjective expressionist gestures can most effectively present a designer's own values they are not necessarily an appropriate way to encapsulate the identity of a global company or to create an environment acceptable to a spectrum of employees. This project, for a branch of an international public relations company, utilises many of the strategies that the designer used in her own office (see pages 142-143), albeit refined by a more objective filter. Both projects do share the same precise use of colour and the same interaction with elements of the existing interior.

The starting point for the colour palette is found in the red of the client's graphic identity and other hues, in which yellow predominates, take it as a tonal reference. The connection is made clear, to staff if not to clients, in the kitchen where not only the branding colour but its 'plus' motif is used to customise cabinets and an equally robust yellow is introduced as the harmonising hue. Walls and ceiling throughout the rest of the building are white with sparse applications of colour in clearly defined and limited locations, on the edges of furniture and the depth of wall recesses. It is only in the zebra triptych and the fragment of pattern derived from it and applied to the base of cupboard doors that blue and green make a modest appearance. Commitment to colour is made clear by the specification of Pantone folding chairs, one of which is hung on a wall like a work of art, its code number displayed to underline the importance attached to colour and the its selection.

Existing interior detail is unexciting but some modest ceiling mouldings survive in a room that has been subdivided to make a meeting place and a corridor that also doubles as a waiting place. To preserve the integrity of the mouldings the new spaces are separated by a glass partition the top of which has a regular pattern of small square cut outs and lines of the ceiling mouldings pass unbroken through four of them. Occupants of both areas see the ceiling decoration in its entirety and its modest appearance is enhanced by this transparent demarcation. Those in the meeting room can enjoy a hard-edged, predominantly black and white, mural on the back wall of the corridor but, when visual separation is necessary, a curtain may be drawn on the corridor side.

TOP
Designed by Anna Butele, the red of the company logo is borrowed for one of the two thematic colours used throughout the interior. The other is yellow. The 'plus' symbol, also borrowed, is only used in the kitchen.

BOTTOM
Plan
1 Entrance
2 Reception
3 Waiting
4 Conference
5 Private office
6 Communal workspace
7 Storage
8 Lavatory

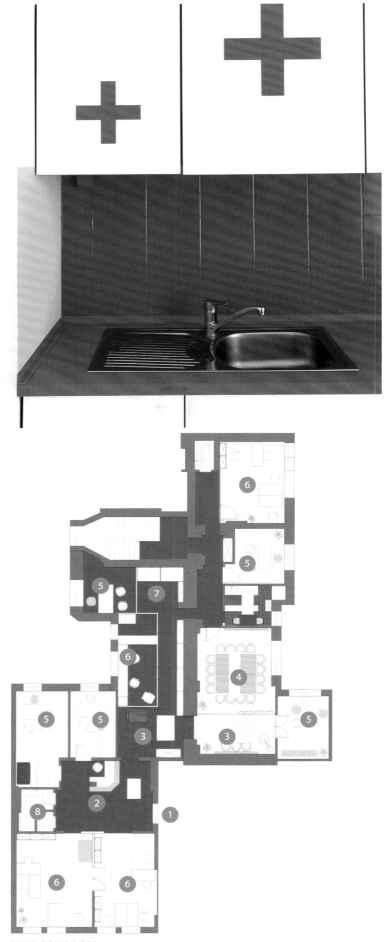

PLAN, SCALE 1:150

TOP LEFT

The red of the logo provides a chromatic reference for other colours used in decorative motifs.

MIDDLE LEFT

The colours and lines of the zebra triptych are applied to the bottom of the cupboard doors.

BOTTOM LEFT

A painted steel frame supports the polished concrete slabs of the table top.

TOP RIGHT

In the meeting room red and yellow bands define the depth of recesses and the edges of the table. The glass partition, cut to allow the original ceiling moulding to remain intact and visible, may be curtained off. It separates the meeting room from the corridor and the mural and projection screen it contains.

BOTTOM RIGHT

The prevailing principle of floating blocks of colour on the otherwise bright white planes is clearly expressed by the wall-hung Pantone folding chair on its yellow ground. The importance of precise colour selection is emphasised by the Pantone code numbers on the chairs. The table support shares the material and angularity of that in the meeting room.

VENTURE 3, LONDON
BRINKWORTH

When it is anticipated that a project will be completed in two phases it is usual for the two to be designed together, to make a single, coherent statement. However, in this project the success and expansion of the client's brand identity company, which coincided with the unexpected availability of space in the same building, offered the opportunity for an objective assessment of the principles that had shaped the original.

The first phase occupied an old squash court on the first floor of a mews building and the new sat immediately below it. The designers were concerned that the new area lacked the spectacular height of the original but realised that, if the former doors in the elevation to the courtyard area were glazed, they would expand the perceived space horizontally, to match the generosity of the upper floor. They also decided that if the major feature of the original, the sloping green wall, were replicated on the lower floor it would connect the two floors and provide the clients with a powerful visual contribution to their own brand identity on the street.

The dark green sloping wall, its colour further deepened by the perforations of the acoustic board that clads it, is the most assertive link between the floors but the deep red, in the upholstery of the chairs and the laminate of the table top, complements it and is equally important in establishing the coherence of the two spaces. The meeting room is given definition and token separation by the frameless, and door-less, glass partitions that divide it from the studio space, making its tonal harmony an integral part of the studio. Red makes a literal connection as it rises through the double-height of the stairwell in which light fittings drop seven metres and match those dropping five metres over the kitchen table. In contrast to the organic rawness of the English oak flooring on both levels the tops of the studio work tables, also on both levels, are finished with a luminous laminate which, when lights are turned off at the end of the day, begin to glow and the device, first deployed on the upper level but now visible from the courtyard, has even greater impact in its second manifestation.

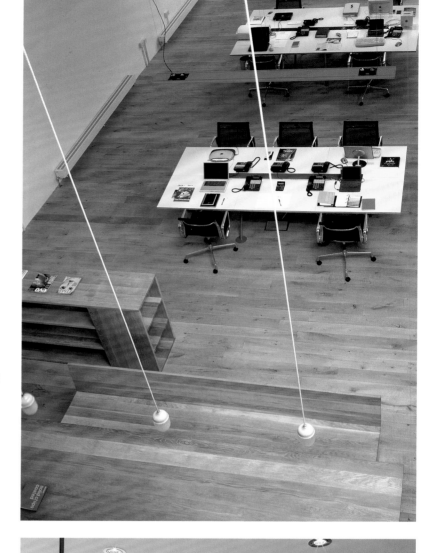

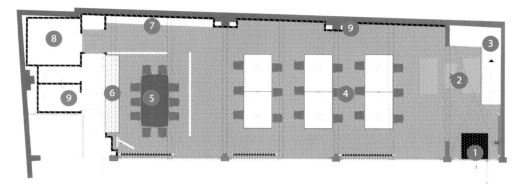

GROUND FLOOR PLAN, SCALE 1:300

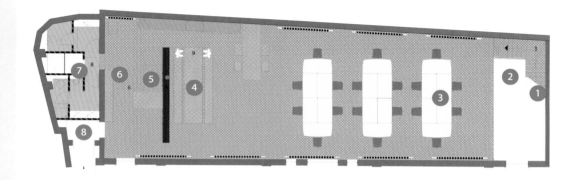

FIRST FLOOR PLAN, SCALE 1:300

TOP
Ground Floor Plan
1 Entrance
2 Reception
3 Stair
4 Worktables
5 Meeting room
6 Sloping acoustic wall
7 Storage
8 Server room
9 Lavatories

MIDDLE
First Floor Plan
1 Stair
2 Void
3 Worktables
4 Kitchen meeting area
5 Sloping acoustic wall
6 Storage
7 Lavatories
8 Fire escape

BOTTOM
Frameless glass walls enclose the meeting room but maintain the visual integrity of the lower level. The red of the table top and chair upholstery matches that in the stairwell.

OPPOSITE TOP
Bench: Side and rear elevation

OPPOSITE MIDDLE LEFT
Section: Bench and Table
1 30mm (1⅕ in) solid oak finger jointed at connection of seat and backrest
2 15mm (⅝ in) solid oak backboard
3 30mm (1⅕ in) solid oak table top
4 70mm (2¾ in) solid oak frame
5 Galvanised foot rest
All timber oil sealed

OPPOSITE LOWER LEFT
Detail A
Galvanised steel angle with blind fixings as shown.

OPPOSITE MIDDLE RIGHT
A galvanised mild steel, square sectioned, footrest compensates for the lofty bench and table and prevents wear to the floor level framing member.

OPPOSITE BOTTOM
Section
1 Green acoustic wall
1 New table and benches
1 Recycled oak bar/library unit
4 Pendant lights hung at two levels
5 Sliding glass screen
6 New opening between reception and studio

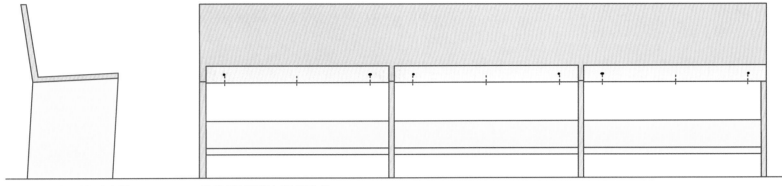

SIDE ELEVATION, SCALE 1:50

REAR ELEVATION, SCALE 1:50

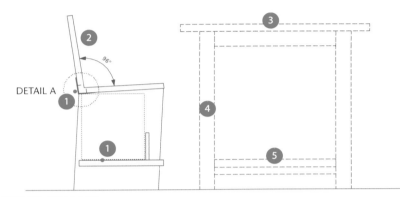

DETAIL A

SECTION, SCALE 1:50

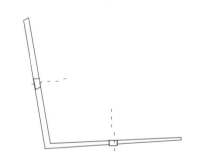

DETAIL A, SCALE 1:25

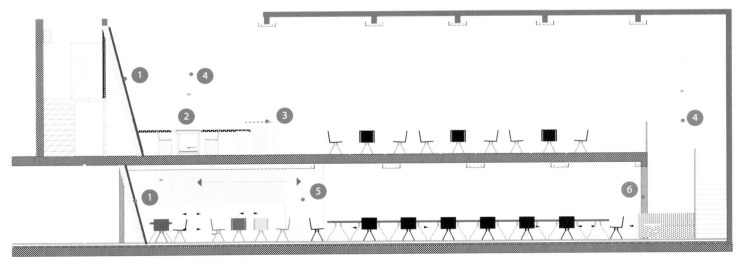

SECTION, SCALE 1:200

STUDENT LOANS COMPANY, GLASGOW
GRAVEN IMAGES

The client is a private company, organising loans on behalf of the government for students undertaking university and college courses in the United Kingdom. Having created an award winning solution for the organisation's offices in the North of England, the designers were asked to refresh its head office, and its twelve hundred strong work force. The most significant physical gesture is the 'inhabited' wall of banquettes, which separate the kitchen, servery and a few tables and chairs from the greater part of the café, an amorphous space given secondary structuring by long tables for casual internet access. The banquette wall deals effectively with the problem of making the least prepossessing area of the room, that furthest from the windows, desirable. Each cubicle offers a semi-private place for social interactions and work-related discussions. The raised floor level allows a defining band to be wrapped around each recess and improves sightlines to the windows beyond. The principle of providing semi-enclosure to make semi-private places is also apparent in the selection of sofas with backs and sides high enough to punctuate, and give identity to, the expanses of anonymous floor elsewhere in the building.

The banquettes are reminiscent of Thomas Jefferson's bed, built into the wall between his bedroom and office and open to both to speed his transition from sleeping to working. This project's fresh interpretation of the principle is perhaps more likely to encourage employees to spend more time in the café but, since the intention is to increase loyalty and motivation, the client calculates that job satisfaction relates to quality of working environment and will increase commitment and productivity. However, while physical improvements provide the desirable working environment that is good for self esteem, the designers also felt it important to reinforce employees' perception of the social value of their work by reminding them that, while arranging loans and pursuing repayments may lack obvious glamour, the process occupies a crucial place in the delivery of higher education. To achieve this they commissioned photographs and printed them large to occupy whole walls of meeting rooms and offices. One series, photographs of venerable university buildings, makes connections to long established traditions. Another series, portraits of beneficiaries of the loan system who have found satisfying careers, offers reassurance of the value of the work.

TOP
Proprietary free-standing furniture creates a similar sense of enclosure and semi-privacy.

MIDDLE
Images of satisfied customers decorate smaller spaces.

BOTTOM
Digitally generated photomurals in meeting rooms borrow the colours, textures and forms of a grander architectural tradition.

ABOVE
The 'inhabited' wall with its integral banquettes divides the island kitchen from the conventional tables and chairs which are further subdivided by the internet shelves

RIGHT
Plan of Restaurant Area
1 Banquette wall
2 Kitchen island
3 Restaurant area
4 Internet shelves
5 Entrance to offices
6 Women's lavatory
7 Men's lavatory

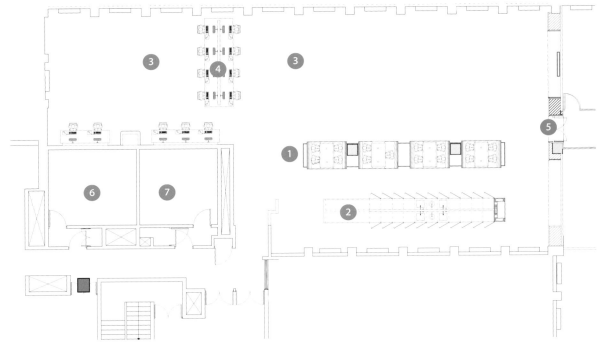

PLAN, SCALE 1:200

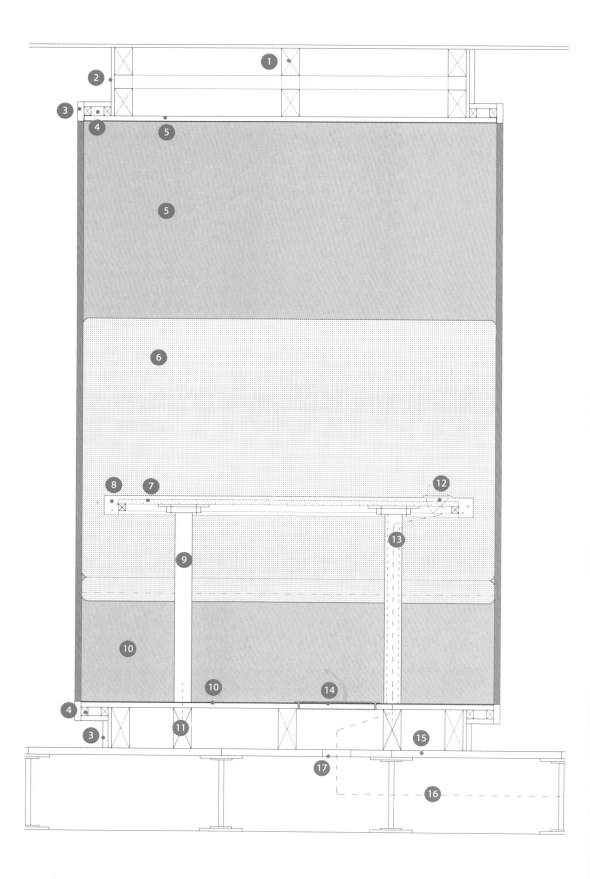

SECTION A-A, SCALE 1:10

LEFT
Section Through Booth
1 Softwood joist to support booth bulkhead and framing
2 Douglas Fir shiplap timber boarding with white oiled finish on 12mm (½ in) plywood backing with concealed fixing to framing
3 Lacquered MDF frame with heavy duty clear lacquer finishing coat
4 Softwood packing as required
5 Fabric covered MDF panel
6 Polyurethane upholstered seat and back pads on dense foam padding fixed to fabric covered MDF panel
7 Matt solid colour core plastic laminate on MDF tabletop with visible underside painted
8 Solid colour core laminate edge
9 Painted square mild steel table leg
10 MDF with 2.5mm (⅛ in) smooth rubber sheet finish
11 Rigid connection between raised deck and base of table leg
12 Anodised aluminium fliptop power and data access point
13 Cable circulation in hollow table leg
14 Removable rubber clad aluminium trimmed MDF access hatch
15 Existing raised floor
16 Power and data cable circulation in raised floor
17 100mm (4 in) diameter hole in raised steel floor panel

OPPOSITE TOP
The banquettes provide semi-private places and beyond them are the more conventional tables, chairs, benches and 'internet shelves' for more informal work and networking.

OPPOSITE MIDDLE
Elevation
1 Fabric clad MDF panel
2 Lacquered MDF frame with heavy duty clear lacquer finishing coat
3 Douglas Fir shiplap timber boarding with white oiled finish on plywood backing
4 Solid colour core plastic laminate on MDF tabletop with visible underside painted
5 Painted 710mm (27½ in) square mild steel table leg
6 Polyurethane upholstered seat and back pads on dense foam padding fixed to fabric covered MDF panel
7 MDF with 2.5mm (⅛ in) smooth rubber sheet finish

OPPOSITE BOTTOM
Plan
1 Existing column
2 Lacquered corner finish
3 Vertical solid timber bead with white oiled finish at corner junctions
4 Recessed power source
5 Downlight

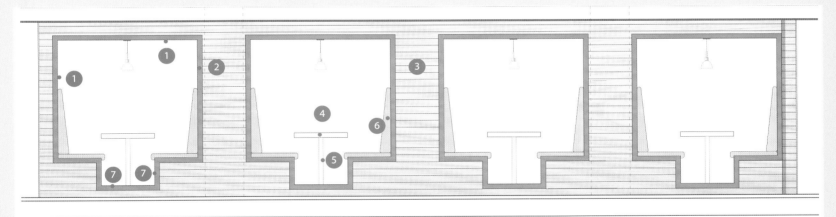

ELEVATION, SCALE 1:50

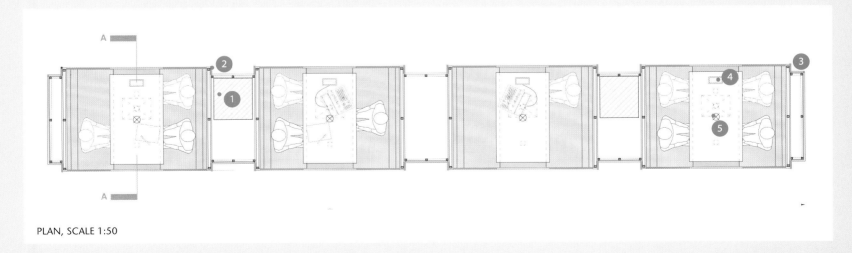

PLAN, SCALE 1:50

ADOBE, LEHI UTAH
RAPT STUDIO

The twenty-five thousand square metres of this new four storey building represents an extremely generous space provision even for its eleven hundred users. It certainly leaves room for physical expansion but also to meet Adobe's request that not only should reflect the company's present identity but should have the capacity to stimulate, and absorb, its evolving culture. Those who own and manage its companies have created a new business and, without deliberate intent, a new business model, and are themselves studiedly informal. Their employees share that instinct, relishing permissive environments in which they may dress as they please and work when they wish. For those who became digitally literate in adolescent online gaming, the line between work and play is blurred. The archetypical digital company interior reflects the ethos and is studiedly un-serious and studiedly un-corporate. So pervasive is the stylistic that its rejection of the clichés of the corporate office has spawned its own clichés. Pinball machines, bean bags and, more recently, playground slides have become de rigeur.

The building's size suggests unlimited possibilities for change. It is enormous but its exterior has the demeanour of a conventional corporate office building and, on entry, the scale of the space and the central structure that sets up conventional corridor routes might be found in a conventional corporate interior. But it is the details that contradict that first impression. The central structure is hollowed out to make meeting rooms and its planes end in acute angles. The circular lobby seats, which would conventionally be generously upholstered, are deconstructed and reconstituted to reveal a construction system of obsessively repetitive ribs and the section of accommodating upholstery is excessively limited when compared to the lengths of concrete, slatted timber and glass seating that make up the fragmented circle.

Obsessive repetition of the upright ribs occurs again on the front of the reception desk, in the slatted ceilings, on the front of the café counter and in the light that hangs above it. It is crucial to the impact of the mural of computer mouses, and for the 'pixillated' gender symbols on lavatory doors. Other pieces of wall art are generated digitally but in the spirit of the alternative is leavened by the work of graffiti artists. It is, however, the view from the entrance of the games hall and café one level below it that best expresses the spirit of the company. It is a 'great indoors', in which pool tables, table-tennis tables and café tables sit isolated in the expanse of floor, which matches the great outdoors of Utah.

RIGHT

Plan: Entrance area
1 Entrance
2 Lobby
3 Composite seating
4 Reception desk
5 Stair to lower social area
6 Meeting rooms
7 Lower social area

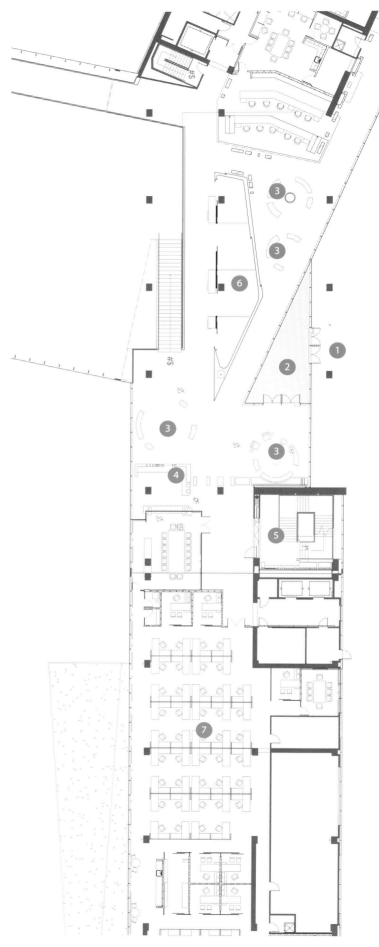

PLAN, SCALE 1:300

ABOVE
A shallow monumental stair connects the expanses of the social area on the lower level with the entrance.

RIGHT
The digitally generated image matches the cavernous scale of the social area.

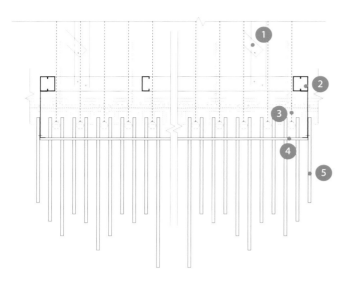

CROSS SECTION, SCALE 1:20

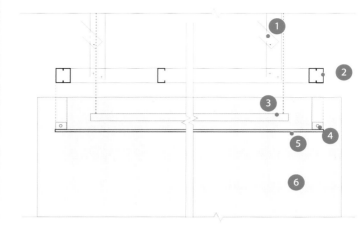

LONG SECTION, SCALE 1:20

TOP LEFT

Cross Section: café counter light
1 62mm (2⅜ in) metal stud braces at 2440mm (100 in) centres
2 Wood grille suspended ceiling
3 Light source
4 Frosted polycarbonate panel
5 Coloured polycarbonate panels

TOP RIGHT

Long Section: café counter light
1 62mm (2⅜ in) metal stud braces at 2440mm (100 in) centres
2 Wood grille suspended ceiling
3 Light source
4 Metal angle and fastener
5 32mm (1¼ in) thick frosted polycarbonate panel
6 Coloured polycarbonate panels to various heights

MIDDLE LEFT

The wooden slats of the suspended ceiling in the café are complemented by the glass fins of the light fitting that hangs above the servery.

LEFT

The ceiling is installed as pre-fabricated panels.

TOP
'Knife edge' conditions

Left: Plan
1 Adjacent partition
2 Fire-resistant timber and MDF blocking
3 Taped, filled and sanded seam between MDF and plasterboard
4 Standard plasterboard and stud partition

Right: Plan
1 Adjacent partition
2 Fire resistant timber and MDF blocking
3 Taped, filled and sanded seam between MDF and plasterboard
4 Furring partition
5 Stainless steel trim
6 White board inset
7 Backing within wall thickness

BOTTOM
The acute prow of the structure that occupies the centre of the office is repeated on a more modest scale along its perimeter.

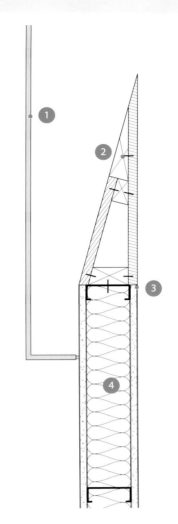

PLAN, SCALE 1:50

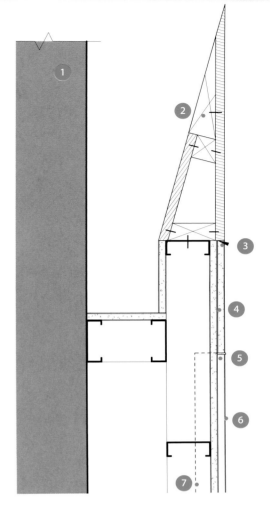

PLAN, SCALE 1:50

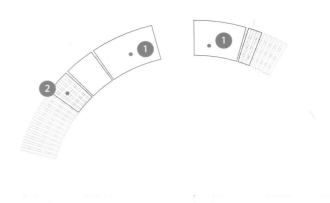

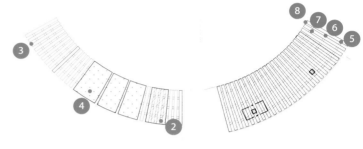

PLAN, SCALE 1:100

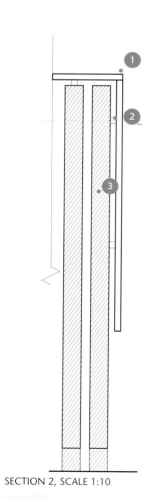

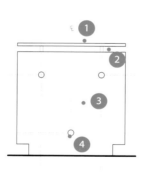

SECTION 1, SCALE 1:50

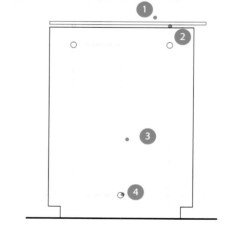

SECTION 2, SCALE 1:10

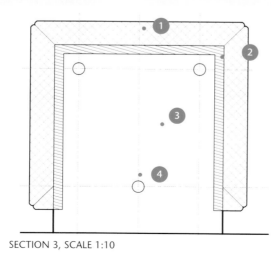

SECTION 3, SCALE 1:10

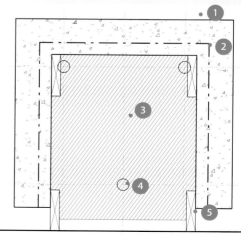

SECTION 4, SCALE 1:10

OPPOSITE TOP AND MIDDLE LEFT

The entrance area is inhabited by fragmented, ribbed circles of seating fashioned from wood, concrete and glass.

OPPOSITE TOP RIGHT

Plan: Typical Circular Bench Seat
1 Pre-cast concrete seats
2 12mm (½ in) fully tempered glass
3 Typical rod end connection
4 Upholstery
5 32mm (1¼ in) slabs
6 Metal rod bent to radius
7 25mm (1 in) metal tubing sleeve
8 19mm (¾ in) spacing at inner edge

OPPOSITE BOTTOM LEFT

Pod Section 2: Glass-topped Table End
1 12mm (½ in) fully tempered glass top
2 12mm (½ in) metal spacers
3 Solid timber support plate

OPPOSITE MIDDLE

Section 1: Glass-topped Table and Bench
1 12mm (½ in) fully tempered glass top
2 12mm (½ in) metal spacers
3 Solid timber support plate
4 25mm (1 in) diameter holes for metal connecting rod

OPPOSITE BOTTOM RIGHT

Section 3: Upholstered Bench
1 Fabric on high density urethane ether foam
2 19mm (¾ in) MDF substrate
3 Solid timber support plate
4 25mm (1 in) diameter holes for metal connecting rod

Section 4: Precast Concrete Seat
1 75mm (3 in) precast concrete seat
2 WWF 25mm (1 in) from inside face of concrete
3 Solid timber support plate
4 25mm (1 in) holes for metal rods
5 Timber runner

TOP LEFT & RIGHT

The building is decorated with texts in different fonts from the Adobe palette and by graffiti artists.

RIGHT

Spray painted computer mouses become decorative devices.

FAR RIGHT

A gender symbol suggests pixellation.

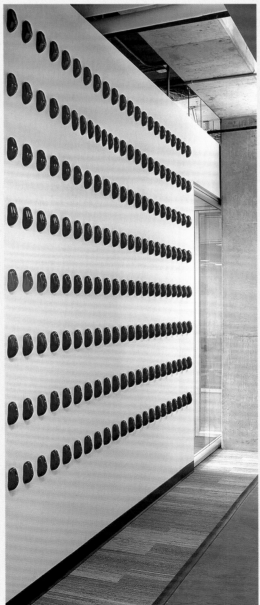

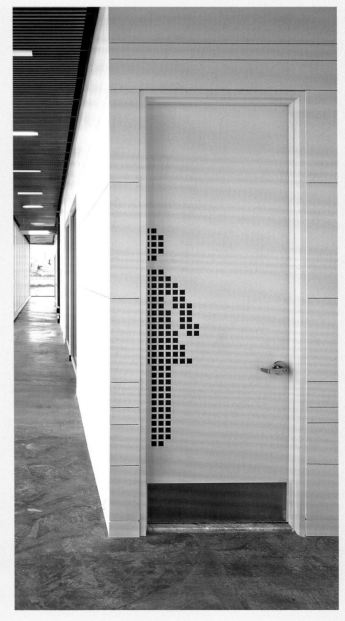

LOGAN,
NEW YORK
SO-IL

For their East Coast office and studio space the media production company Logan chose a corner 'loft' space on the first floor of a protected building in the centre of the SoHo district. The design is a response to the company's operating structure in which a large proportion of those working on any particular project are employed only for its duration and that volatility pointed to the importance of promoting a sense of collaboration and collectivity amongst a peripatetic work force. The fluid structure did not suggest a solution of personalised workstations and private rooms, both of which would establish an unproductive demarcation between permanent and temporary staff.

Strategic planning suggested that the floor space should be divided into two rooms and these are separated by a double skin of tightly stretched translucent fabric, which subsumes a line of structural columns. Diffused images of columns, and the windows and radiators that sit in the space between the fabric and the external walls, remain visible. The intensity and tint of natural light changes throughout the day. Pale figures are visible through the screens but no shadows are cast by the stretched PVC luminous ceiling that bathes each room in an even light.

Fluctuations in the size of groups requires a high degree of flexibility and both rooms are defined by a custom built table, nineteen and a half metres long, which is capable of supporting individual and group activities with equal efficiency and is free of any indicators, other than evenly spaced power points, of individual or collective territories. Glass screens divide off, physically but not visually, the end sections of both tables that are nearest the external wall, to create acoustically private rooms for meetings and discreet conversations. Commitment to symmetry is paramount and each enclosed space has two doors, which does have the practical advantage of eliminating circumnavigations of the table. Privacy is consolidated by glass screens set within the fabric skins of fabric between adjacent rooms, although may occasionally be compromised by the en fillade planning that requires users of one office to enter through the other. Ancilliary and specialist functions are accommodated in the L-shaped perimeter floor area that wraps around the communal rooms. Felt lined walls acoustically isolate sound editing suites.

TOP
Stretched translucent fabric walls filter light and images.

MIDDLE
Existing columns sit between the double skins of wall fabric.

LOW MIDDLE
A single table occupies the centre of the two communal work rooms.

BOTTOM
Glass partitions cut the table to create smaller spaces without destroying the idea of a single space and continuous table.

ABOVE AND RIGHT
The tables form nuclei for large project teams but accommodate smaller groups and individuals as effectively.

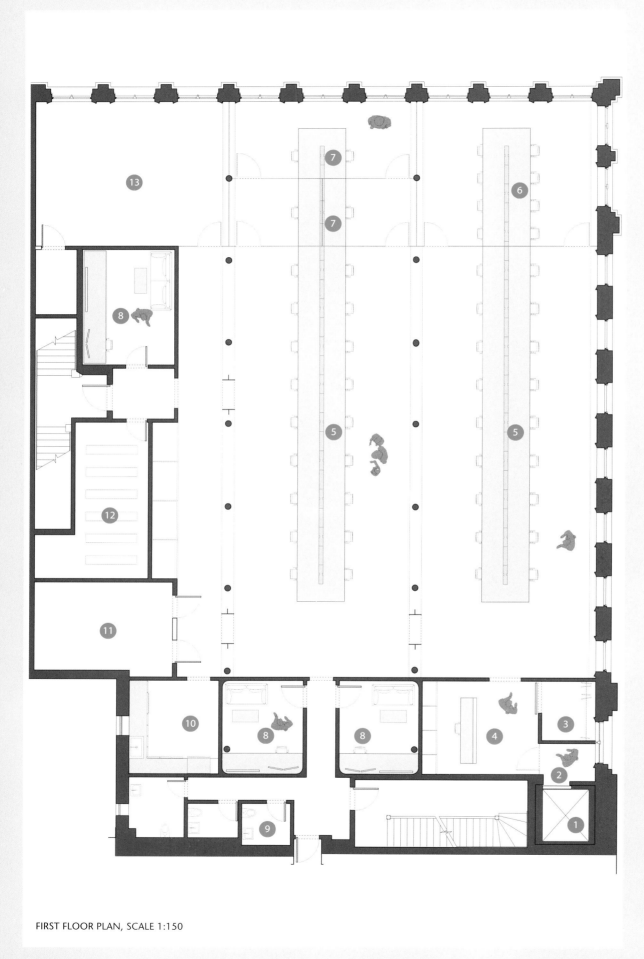

FIRST FLOOR PLAN, SCALE 1:150

LEFT
Plan
1 Lift
2 Entrance vestibule
3 Cloakroom
4 Reception
5 Work stations
6 Conference room
7 Office
8 Editing bay
9 Lavatory
10 Kitchen
11 Mechanical plant room
12 Server room
13 Recording room

OPPOSITE TOP
The smaller spaces provide a degree of quiet without isolation. A glass partition, set between the fabric skins improves acoustic isolation.

OPPOSITE BOTTOM
Felt lined walls provide acoustic separation in the editing suites.

TELETECH CALL CENTRE AND INCUBATOR, DIJON
MVRDV

Call centres are popularly perceived to be among the least desirable of work places and multi-storey factory buildings, built and abandoned in the very recent past, are not credited with the gritty glamour of older industrial building shells. This conversion, of redundant mustard factory to call centre, contradicts both presumptions and, more significantly, suggests how the job may be made desirable. It demonstrates that abandoned but weather proof building stock, however unprepossessing, can be resuscitated productively and that, with ubiquitous digital connections assumptions about how and where people work are there to be challenged.

Teletech is a French service provider, with call centres across the world, which invests significantly in its social policy with the intention of attracting and retaining good quality staff who will, in turn, improve interaction with consumers. This call centre has predictable busy periods spread across the day and only at these times need the centre be fully staffed. The transforming strategy is that, outside of those periods, employees may make use of an education centre, a fitness centre, a gallery and an incubator space for personal projects. Investment in these areas has meant that elsewhere the budget often only allowed the removal or the painting of existing elements but the potential of the existing atrium, mezzanine, windows and roof lights has been exploited to make basic but special social spaces.

Perhaps even more radical is the rethinking of how people might choose to work. The underlying premise is that the young, who make up the majority of call centre staff, are accustomed to working with laptops on, for example, sofas or beds, to sprawl rather than to sit in the manner prescribed by ergonomic data. Rooms of cubicles for individual operators are, presently, retained but the alternative allows workers to log in anywhere in the building, in quiet places, wide open expanses or secluded corners. The principal area for this optional work style is the double-height space on the third floor in which tiers of timber boarding, detailed with economic prudence to match the simplicity of the existing building, allow workers to occupy their place of choice in the manner of their choosing. The difference in level between tiers provides a comfortable seating height or workers can use one of the stylish, very casual, chairs scattered across the area. Exotic chairs and chandeliers in the void over the entrance hall are the only overt attempts to suggest glamour but the opportunity to inhabit, in a proprietorial fashion, the near blank canvases of extraordinary empty volumes gives staff the seductive possibility of shaping their own working lives.

TOP
The existing façade was upgraded by a QR flashcode pattern that communicates the activities of the company and signals the transformation of the interior.

ABOVE
The use of a single colour for the floor, walls and ceiling in the modest volume of the second floor canteen shows the restraint that characterises the grander spaces.

OPPOSITE TOP
Wooden plateaus convert huge interior volumes into a 'landscape' in which workers can find their preferred space, working on laptops, sitting where they want, how they want. The same areas may be used for recreation outside busy work times.

OPPOSITE BOTTOM
Section
1 'Landscaped' work area
2 Void
3 Conventional call centre provision
4 Bicycle parking
5 Car parking

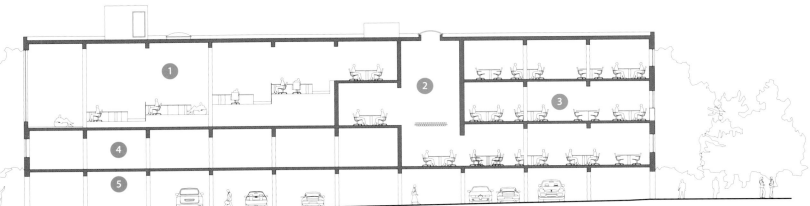

SECTION, SCALE 1:300

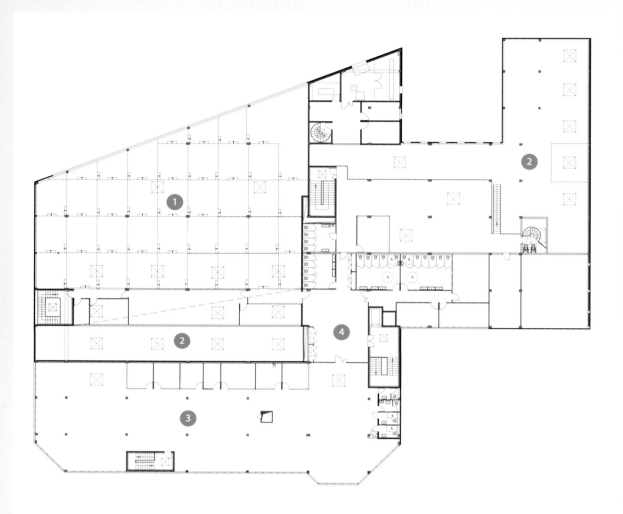

PLAN, SCALE 1:400

LEFT
Plan
1 'Landscaped' work area
2 Void
3 Conventional call centre provision
4 Lobby

BOTTOM LEFT
While light fittings have the scale of chandeliers and provide an ironic glamour, the loops of electric cable that hang beneath them show affinity with the utilitarian simplicity of the former industrial interior.

BOTTOM MIDDLE
Existing windows connect the new internal landscape to the natural elements that border the site.

BOTTOM RIGHT
The use of a single colour for the floor, walls and ceiling in the more modest volume of the second floor canteen shows the restraint that characterises the grander spaces

OPPOSITE TOP
Where enclosure is necessary elements are rigorously self-effacing.

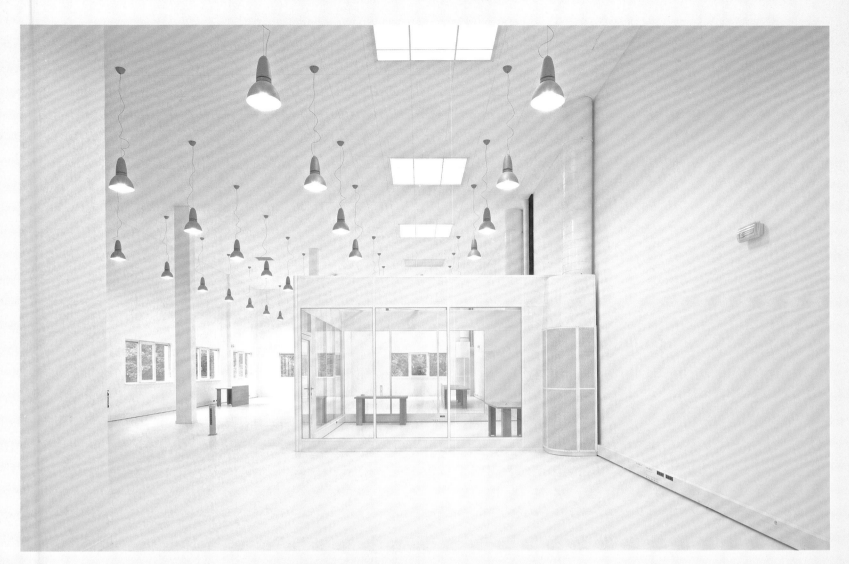

GLASGOW LIFE, GLASGOW
GRAVEN IMAGES

The public sector has learnt from the private the importance of asserting their presence and principles to clients and customers. They have also seen that the more progressive and productive private companies have found ways to encourage cohesion and collective endeavour among their staff by recognising that digital technology has changed how people work, that the tools of their trade have become the tools of their social lives and that boundaries between work and relaxation have blurred. They have learnt from those examples that satisfied employees may be trusted to balance recreation against weight of work.

This project was concerned with rationalising and upgrading one new and five existing city centre buildings to accommodate three thousand five hundred council employees more efficiently, to increase productivity and to make significant cost savings. There was not necessarily a universal solution for the six sites but, given that there is one truly right answer for a single problem it is not surprising that analysis of very similar working methods and of the interactions within and between departments came to a single conclusion. From that research evolved a concept of 'agile working'; providing flexible and practical workspaces for teams and individuals. Further consideration of the position of the individual employee suggested that fluid, and potentially unsettling, working conditions would be more acceptable if each location had a core social area, essentially, perhaps inevitably, a café and a breakout area. In all locations these are organised around a bank of two or three banquettes that define a boundary or a focus for an area of more conventional café tables and chairs. The banquettes sit invitingly on circulation routes, acknowledging that refreshment and socialising are part of the experience of the working day. Behind the banquettes, sandwiched between high cupboards that include recycling bins, is a run of kitchen units for preparing drinks and snacks.

Other standard components, reception desks, waiting benches and office furniture are also common to each location, with variations in colour and pattern that respond to the particularities of context. The older buildings present trickier planning problems, both strategic and tactical, but their grander detailing adds to their identity. In the blander modern shells graphics, sometimes text and sometimes digitally enhanced photographs are deployed to enrich walls, both solid and transparent. Text reminds employees about their obligations and encourage their aspirations. Photographs foster pride with wall-sized celebratory images of the city.

RIGHT
Colours of upholstery and laminates vary in each location but the basic configuration of banquettes remains consistent.

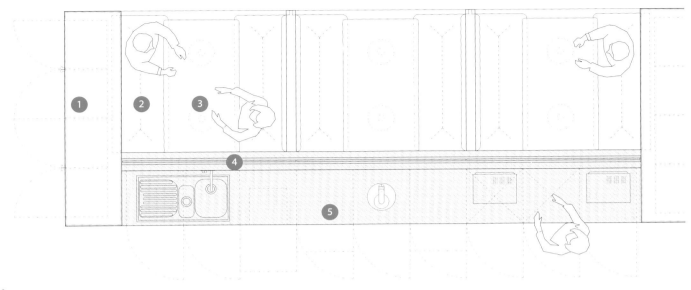

PLAN, SCALE 1:40

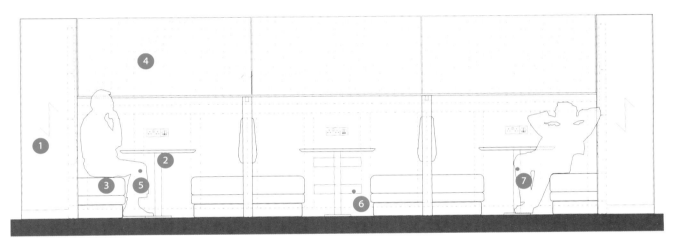

ELEVATION, SCALE 1:40

TOP
Banquette Plan
1 Cupboards with integrated waste collection
2 Bench
3 Table
4 Clear acrylic screen
5 Kitchen worktop

MIDDLE
Banquette Elevation
1 Cupboard end
2 Table
3 Bench
4 Clear acrylic screen
5 Broken lines indicate softwood structure to screen
6 Stainless steel ventilation grille
7 Brushed stainless steel fixed pedestal base

BOTTOM
Axonometric

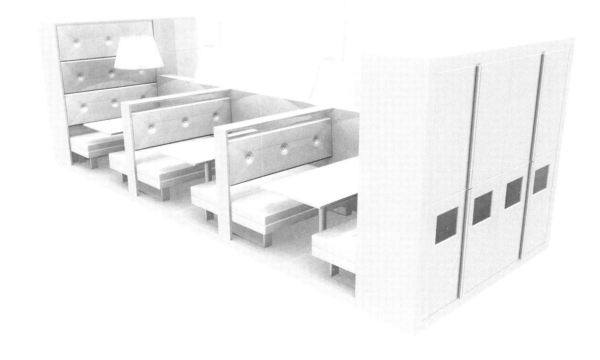

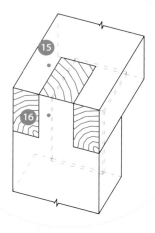

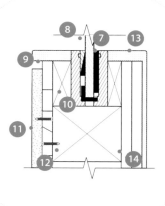

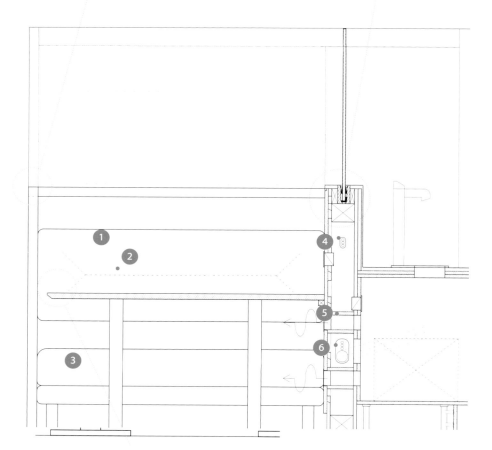

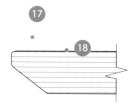

Section through Bench and Kitchen Units
1 Upholstered panels
2 Stitching detail
3 Upholstered backrest and seat
4 Holes in softwood frame for electrical cable circulation
5 Duct with grill to banquette to ventilate under counter boiler unit
6 Holes in softwood frame for water and drainage circulation

Screen and Upstand Detail
7 Aluminium fixing channel
8 15mm (⅝ in) clear acrylic with applied vinyl graphics
9 15mm (⅝ in) shadow gap – visible area of plywood substrate painted to match panel – visible area of vertical panel finished with matching melamine strip
10 Softwood packing
11 18mm (¾ in) melamine faced chipboard panel on split batten fixings with 15mm (⅝ in) shadow gap at panel joints painted to match panels
12 Internal softwood frame
13 Acrylic based composite finish to top and face of upstand with 5mm pencil rounded on exposed edges
14 Plywood substrate

Timber Joint Detail
15 Corner lap joint
16 5mm (⅕ in) spray painted mild steel bar fitted to routered corner on rear face of timber rails and fixed to floor and wall panels

Table Edge Detail
17 Laminate table top finish
18 30mm (1⅕ in) birch plywood table with exposed and chamfered ply edge

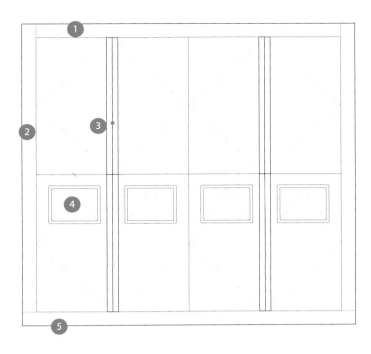

ELEVATION, SCALE 1:20

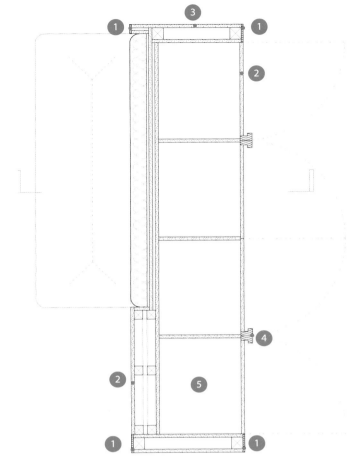

PLAN, SCALE 1:20

TOP LEFT

Cupboard elevation
1 Oak cornice trim
2 Oak edge trim
3 Double oak pull handles
4 Stainless steel flip bin lid
5 Oak skirting trim

TOP RIGHT

Cupboard plan
1 Stained and lacquered oak facing
2 18mm (¾ in) melamine faced
chipboard panel
3 Stained and lacquered oak veneer on
18mm (¾ in) MDF board
4 Stained and lacquered oak handle
5 Melamine faced chipboard for all
internal cupboard surfaces

RIGHT

Cupboard section
1 Stained and lacquered oak facing
2 Dense fire retardant foam
3 Fire retardant fabric upholstery on high
level panels with stitching detail
4 Fire retardant fabric upholstery on seat
and backrest with stitching detail
5 Brushed stainless steel flat bar bent to
form base for seating support
6 Melamine faced chipboard doors with
matching PVC edging strips
7 Melamine faced chipboard shelves with
matching PVC edging strips
8 Stainless steel bin flap
9 Stained and lacquered oak full height
pull handle
10 Oak skirting

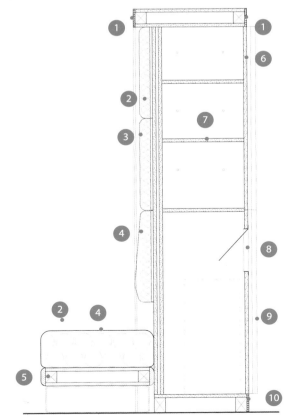

SECTION, SCALE 1:20

LEFT
The reception desk, with a lowered section and knee space for wheel chair users, is common to all locations.

MIDDLE
Corporate exhortations provide raw material for decorative panels.

BOTTOM LEFT & RIGHT
Digitally enhanced images of local landmarks distinguish social areas.

OPPOSITE TOP
Adhesive vinyl on glass walls, with imagery digitally derived from motifs on the city's coat of arms, provides varying degrees of privacy.

OPPOSITE BOTTOM LEFT & RIGHT
The colour of the wall behind the bench and the vinyl panels on the doors vary on each level.

NETLIFE RESEARCH, OSLO
ERIKSEN SKAJAA ARCHITECTS

Netlife is a 'user-experience' consultancy, creating user friendly experiences principally in the fields of human-computer interaction, web and graphic design. They wanted a reassessment of their offices and specifically asked for new spaces for reflective and creative thinking. Their designers tackled the first task pragmatically but for the second they thought more metaphorically. The conventional offices occupy deep, dark spaces with modest headroom. To alleviate this white ceilings are paired with white rubber floors. Wide translucent glass walls, lit from within, make up two walls of each new meeting room. The other walls to the meeting rooms are transparent glass and allow the illuminated walls to spill across the wide circulation routes. Each meeting room has its own shallow fascia and ceiling/roof, which sit visually independent of the service conduits and structural beams above them. Each room is also visually separated from the floor by strip light concealed in a raised perimeter strip.

There are four metaphorical spaces, designated 'gardens' by the designers. All are given identity by retrained allusions to tranquil places. The intention is not to create bogus environments but to evoke the idea of a place that is conducive to reflection and creativity. In the 'kitchen' area the natural wood of the rustic chairs amidst white elements, made the harsher by the black walls that enclose them. Timber lipping on the round tables is the fragile bridge between chairs and whiteness. A 'kitchen garden' is implied by a modest collection of herbs, underneath a light that nurtures photosynthesis, that are, like the chairs, no more than signifiers. The 'forest clearing' is more substantial but paradoxically more abstract. Timber planks, hung from the ceiling, suggest tree trunks but also physically enclose an area for socialising. Green upholstered furniture adds to the conceit. The most substantial of the metaphors is the 'monastery' a white-pigmented birch plywood clad box, constructed around remnants of existing brick walls that also determine the subdivision of rooms, intended as places of retreat and solitary contemplation, within it. The exterior of the box is punctured by round headed openings of varying sizes and at various heights that act as entrances, unglazed windows and seats but principally as niches for pot plants. It does evoke the idea of a monastery and its awkward simplification of motif and detail, added to the incongruity of its context, give it a potency that a more literal pastiche would have lacked.

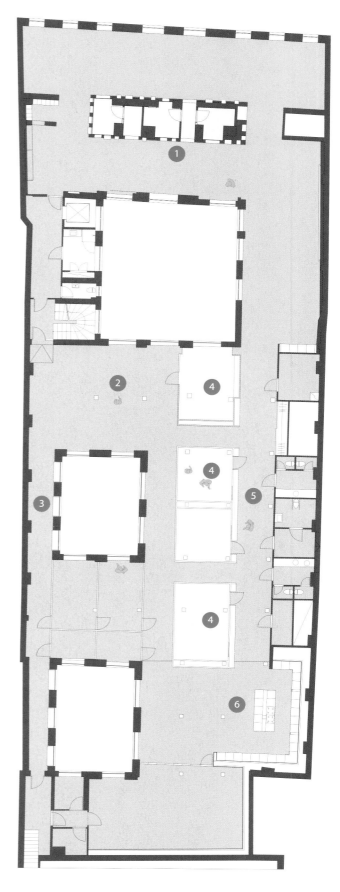

PLAN, SCALE 1:150

RIGHT
Plan
1 The monastery
2 Lounge
3 Corridor with reading recesses
4 Meeting rooms
5 Black corridor
6 Kitchen

TOP LEFT
A white rubber floor, white painted ceiling and light boxes that serve as partitions between meeting rooms counteract the low, windowless space.

TOP RIGHT
The black walled corridor between banks of meeting rooms provides a counterpoint to the white work spaces.

MIDDLE
Meeting rooms appear to float free of floor and ceiling on a concealed light source at skirting level.

BOTTOM
In the kitchen and eating area traditional chairs, with natural wooden frames and woven rush seats, designate a place for reflection amongst the white painted walls and existing steel columns.

TOP LEFT
The kitchen 'garden', like the other organic metaphors, relies for its impact on the extreme contrast between its modest physical presence and the white hard edged space in which it sits.

TOP RIGHT
Lengths of natural wood hang from the ceiling to enclose the 'forest clearing' refuge.

BOTTOM
The white tinted plywood cladding of the 'monastery' provides the most private reflection spaces. Shadow gaps suggest that the structure floats free of both floor and ceiling.

TOP
Round headed openings suggest the doors, windows and niches of a medieval monastic building.

BOTTOM LEFT
Simple furniture in narrow rooms suggests a monk's cell.

BOTTOM RIGHT
Extended window frames provide places to sit and are reminiscent of the low walls between the columns of a medieval cloister.

ZAPATA Y HERRERA, VALENCIA
MASQUESPACIO

For this small lawyers' office in a nineteenth century building in the historic centre of Valencia the designers wanted to avoid using the formal and traditional trappings of professional status while still implying their clients' serious intent and efficiency. The finished interior is low key with no evidence of extravagant spending that might intimidate some potential clients. It speaks of no-frills efficiency. Furniture is elegant, but not extravagant. Light grey walls and ceiling and mid grey floors provide a neutral backdrop in all areas. Clear glazed partitions in black metal frames open up vistas in the low and comparatively modest floor area. Only the trainees are hidden away, behind walls that do not quite reach the ceiling.

The designers use the existing wooden ceiling beams, which have been restored and are visible in all areas of the office, to signify solid traditional values. They have no qualms however about suspending ductwork below them and the stainless steel tubular sections make a link between the rhetoric of the beams and the utilitarian artefacts of the working office below them.

Solid wood is reiterated in the steps that lead down from the front door to the timber-fronted reception desk. The treads are angled to orientate clients away from the partners' glass walled offices to the waiting area beyond it. Wood is also the material used for some witty wall decorations. The first, directed against professional pomposity, is a collage of rectangles, some natural wood, some painted black, that hangs on the wall of the meeting room, in the sightline of anyone descending the entrance steps. The rectangles refer to the frames of the diplomas and certificates that are customarily displayed on the walls of most lawyers' offices and suggest that qualifications may be nothing without experience and commitment to clients' interests. The second wall piece, a version of which is hung in the waiting area and the private office that is without an external window, consists of strips of wood, some natural and some painted grey that hang from a horizontal batten, which is itself suspended from the ceiling. These bring texture and light and shade to the otherwise blank plaster surface but they also suggest vertical wooden blinds, which might be concealing a window to the outside.

RIGHT
Original beams have been restored and prompt the use of wood throughout the new interior. Walls are light grey and furniture and fittings black.

PLAN, SCALE 1:100

LEFT
Plan
1 Entrance
2 Reception desk
3 Meeting room
4 Shared office
5 Individual office
6 Waiting room
7 Store
8 Lavatory
9 'Garden'

BOTTOM LEFT
The wooden rectangles that make the low relief decoration on the boardroom wall represent the diplomas and professional certifications that normally festoon the walls of lawyers' offices.

BOTTOM MIDDLE
Strips, some natural wood finish, others grey, hang from a wooden horizontal, itself suspended from the ceiling. Their role is decorative one but they also suggest vertical venetian blinds and a window to the room.

BOTTOM RIGHT
A private office: table tops rest on storage units to maximise the use of space. The black timber hanging rail reworks one of the project's themes.

OPPOSITE TOP
Cantilevered tables line three sides of the space for junior staff. The air conditioning ducts are as visually significant as the timber beams.

EMU FILMS, LONDON
STUDIO SWINE

It is frequently, and convincingly, argued that a tough site and/ or a limited budget will bring out the best in designers because, to achieve something of merit, they will be forced to rely on raw creativity and to develop unfamiliar options. Acquiescent building shells and accommodating budgets encourage the replication, with nominal re-tuning, of ideas that belong in other contexts. For this project a small film production company, keen to be located in the centre of London's film making district, was prepared to sacrifice space to find an affordable property and, within the ten square metres of awkwardly shaped plan, they wanted work places for up to four people. They found a young design company happy to take on the smallest job and keen to investigate unfamiliar options.

The finished interior speaks of ingenuity rather than expediency and of an inspired use of resources, values appreciated by potential investors. Planning is simple and demonstrably sensible, three people could, just, work at the long table and the fold-down table and fold-up chair that fits beside it accommodates the fourth. The use of recycled elements demonstrate social responsibility but also bring a story that gives the modest room character. The top of the (comparatively) long table is a fragment of mahogany parquet flooring from a local school and the lichen and bark covered shelves are from oak trees, sustainably produced near to London, and are radial offcuts, in effect the waste material from the processing of tree trunks into regularly dimensioned planks.

The wooden pieces are the overt signs of environmental thinking but the other major material, linoleum, is equally virtuous, produced from ninety seven per cent natural materials and is used conventionally to tile the floor and, more idiosyncratically, to upgrade visually mundane but efficient items of office furniture. While the floor tiles mimic the pattern of marble, the scraps used to face the ends of box files and cabinet drawers sport more racy patterns and colours. These flamboyant pieces are also used to make a collection of one off pockets that hold pens and paper clips and the other small necessities of a functioning office. They adopt the principles of origami and flat packed cardboard boxes. Lines of folds are incised to ensure precision and pieces are connected with loose stitching. Their charm lies partly in the wholly comprehensible, flagrantly simple processes behind their conception and production.

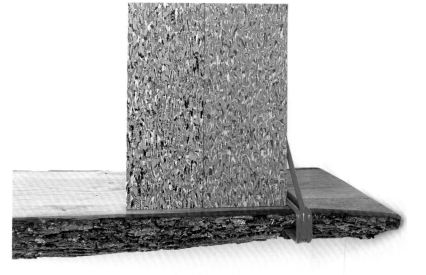

TOP
Grooves are cut into the thickness of the lichen covered oak shelves to accommodate the metal bracket supports. Plywood box files are faced with strips of Marmoleon.

RIGHT
The Marmoleon pattern matches the texture of the oak.

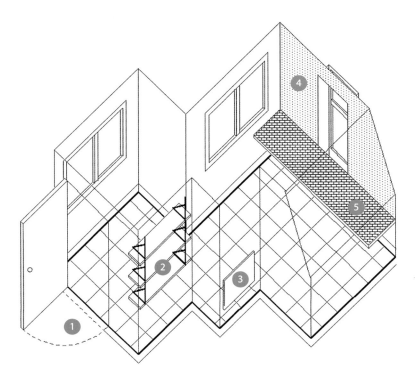

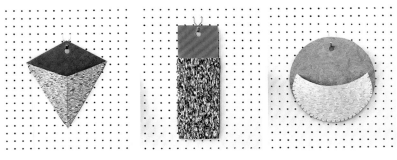

TOP
Axonometric view
1 Entrance
2 Log shelves
3 Folding table
4 Pegboard wall
5 Parquet table top

TOP RIGHT
Peg boarding provides support for ready made and custom made equipment. The table top, salvaged parquet flooring is supported at its mid point by a Marmoleon fronted filing cabinet.

ABOVE
Pieces of Marmoleon are cut to shape, folded and stitched to make storage pouches that are hung from the pegboard by proprietary hooks.

BOTTOM
Laminate faced plywood brackets, with a cut out finger slot, folds out to support a laminate faced plywood table top.

HYPERNUIT, PARIS
H2O ARCHITECTES

The client employs a peripatetic workforce of freelance specialists in artistic direction, graphic design and public relations, each of whom is likely to work exclusively and independently on a single project. The brief asked for five similarly sized desks, a meeting room and modest kitchen and lavatory provision. The street level site offered ample floor area but posed the familiar problems of distributing natural light throughout the volume and ensuring an appropriate degree of privacy for each workstation. The single glazed wall effectively extended the perceived boundaries of the space and offered the opportunity to endow the agency with a distinctively radical identity to the street. The designers chose to blur the precise definition of the enclosure further by introducing ostensibly random angles into detailed planning and by deconstructing each workstation and piling its constituent elements high to imply a random assembly of disparate elements. These formed a secondary, heavily modelled barrier that presented a richer, more ambiguous elevation to the street and opened up complex views to the core of each workstation. The width and height of the composite units give each a protective edge and a degree of privacy appropriate to the needs of itinerant specialist workers engaged in individual projects.

All workstation components were fabricated off site to minimise installation delays but precise fitting on site has absorbed the few irregularities of the existing plan. The grey of the principal components matches that of the floor to create a primarily monolithic composition which is enlivened by the white finish of the exposed cores of various storage units. Existing surfaces are painted white but perimeter planes are broken by panels, of standard grey and varying heights, which line visible wall areas. Books and objects brought by each worker add random patches of colour.

The meeting room is partly tucked behind a length of solid exterior wall and further distanced from the street by the sloping pavement which sets it on a low plinth. A canted wall of cupboards internally shields it and the gaps left at the exterior window and ceiling are closed by frameless glass panels. A solid white sliding door allows the room to be integrated with the central space when appropriate. It boasts the office's one light shade, which contrasts with the exposed bulbs that hang above each workstation, but its existing walls and planted panels conform to tonal principles.

PLAN, SCALE 1:100

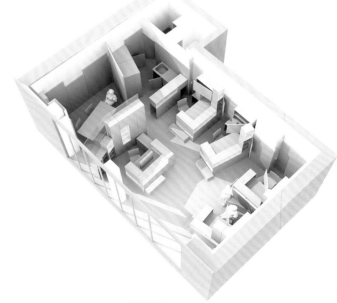

TOP
The considered layout and organisation of workstations is not apparent in the seemingly random assemblages of storage components that are visible from the street.

MIDDLE
Plan
1 Entrance
2 Work station
3 Meeting room
4 High level glazing strip

5 Sliding door
6 Kitchen
7 Lavatory
8 Clothes storage

BOTTOM
Model
The high level glazing that seals off the meeting room on the far left is clearly visible.

TOP LEFT
The rationale of workstation modules is apparent in the interior. The open sliding door reveals the interior of the meeting room.

TOP RIGHT
Signs of habitation add colour and irregularities to the monotonic assemblages.

BOTTOM LEFT
Modules fit together precisely but the effect is of casual stacking. The naked light bulbs reinforce the impression of a temporary installation.

BOTTOM RIGHT
In the meeting room shelving units fill the recess between column and door. Wall panels of different heights continue the irregular top edge that characterises all modular assemblies.

STUDIO APPOLLONI, BARCELONA
BARBARA APPOLLONI

This project, in the shell of a former electrical repair workshop, began with demolition. A mezzanine over the street entrance was removed to let in sunlight and a second, at the rear, was cut back and part of its steel frame retained to support storage elements beside and above the new kitchen area. What is now the courtyard had been enclosed as a storage shed and its roof was removed.

Once the shell had been stripped of its less desirable accretions the long thin volume required no subdivision. A few practical, and photogenic, furniture pieces, a long workbench complete with vice, a little wall-mounted drawer unit and a 'fifties wall-mounted task light were retained. The raw and battered wooden bench is matched on the opposite wall by a continuous run of shelves which is punctuated by three pairs of worktables at right angles to it. These shelves and tables define the function and character of the new interior and their aesthetic draws on the spirit of the simple traditional detailing of the wooden framed door and window screen to the street. Constructed from standard sheets of MDF they necessarily avoid even the simple mouldings of the screen but the play of light on the slight projections of plane, on the narrow edges that project beyond recessed expanses gives enough surface modulation to match the play of light on the screen's mouldings. The unaligned rectangles of shelving have an affinity with the informal pattern of large and small windows and their dark flat colour is close to that of the screen. The deep red of the short section of bench, a nominal waiting place, energises the run of shelving.

The kitchen and storage cupboard may be shut away behind two tall sliding doors, each with a full height wooden pull handle that tapers away from its central round finger slot towards top and bottom edges. The wooden storage boxes that sit above the kitchen and cupboard were also salvaged from the old workshop. The bespoke wheeled meeting table, with its oak legs and top of local stone, is bulky enough to hold its own against the old bench.

The steel framed doors to the courtyard are new. The lavatory is new but in the same position as one in the demolished storage shed. Its new enclosure of corrugated metal sheet, which is supported on an inner wall of lightweight concrete blocks and is continued to mask the unsightly condition of the existing perimeter wall. The roof of the lavatory will be planted to create a very small urban garden.

TOP
Repairs to the original wooden façade draw on the modest traditional detail of the original but a louvre window fixed horizontally indicates a fresh pragmatism.

RIGHT
The colour of the new façade continues in the interior on the painted MDF shelving that runs the length of one side wall.

TOP LEFT

A cushioned bench is set into the run of shelving. The slight projection of uprights beyond the front of the top panel adds detail that matches the restraint of the original façade.

TOP RIGHT

The red bench punctuates and enlivens the run of shelving.

MIDDLE

The table's end panel continues the detailing principles of the shelves.

BELOW

Plan
1 Work space
2 Bench/waiting
3 Meeting space
4 Kitchen
5 Storage
6 Lavatory
7 Patio

BOTTOM

Elevation: Bench Wall
1 Security screen housing
2 Wall-mounted light
3 Change in paint colour
4 Suspended light track
5 Reclaimed drawer unit
6 Reclaimed work bench
7 Wall-mounted spotlight
8 Sliding door track
9 Kitchen
10 Sliding door (storage behind)
11 Lavatory
12 Wall cladding

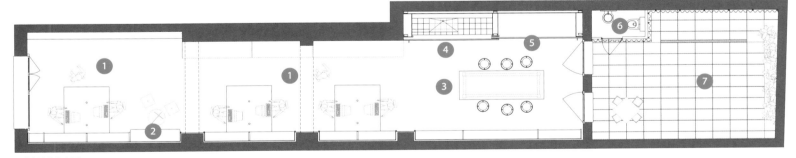

PLAN, SCALE 1:100

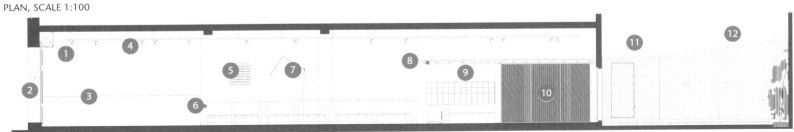

ELEVATION, SCALE 1:100

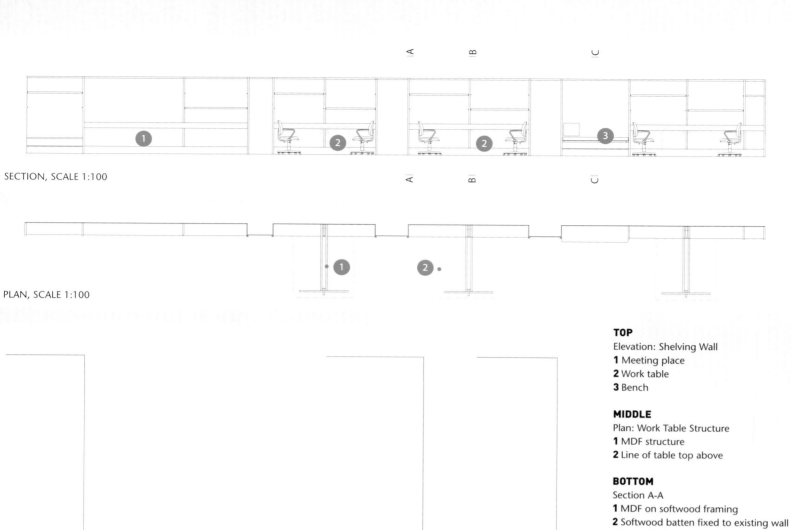

SECTION, SCALE 1:100

PLAN, SCALE 1:100

TOP
Elevation: Shelving Wall
1 Meeting place
2 Work table
3 Bench

MIDDLE
Plan: Work Table Structure
1 MDF structure
2 Line of table top above

BOTTOM
Section A-A
1 MDF on softwood framing
2 Softwood batten fixed to existing wall
3 MDF side and back panels
4 MDF shelf
5 MDF on softwood framing
6 Existing wall
All MDF surfaces painted

Section B-B
1 MDF on softwood framing
2 Softwood batten fixed to existing wall
3 MDF side and back panels
4 MDF shelf on dowel supports
5 Dowel shelf supports
6 MDF on softwood framing shelf
7 MDF table top
8 Paired MDF frame
9 Single MDF frame
10 MDF panel
11 MDF shelf
12 MDF on softwood framing
13 Existing wall
All MDF surfaces painted

Section C-C
1 MDF on softwood framing
2 Softwood batten fixed to existing wall
3 MDF side and back panels
4 MDF shelf on dowel supports
5 Dowel shelf supports
6 MDF on softwood framing shelf
7 MDF shelf
8 MDF on softwood framing
9 Existing wall
All MDF surfaces painted

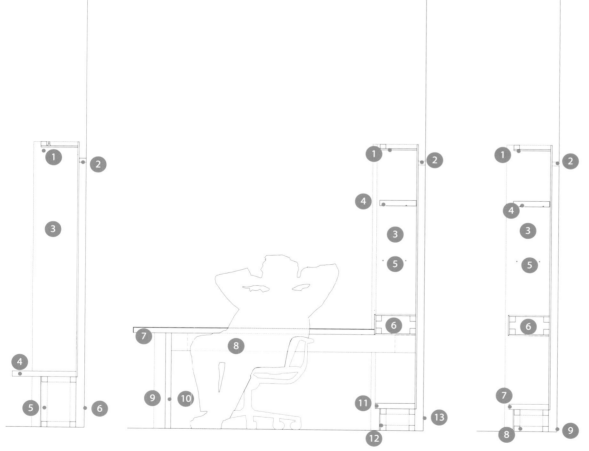

SECTION A-A, SCALE 1:25   SECTION B-B, SCALE 1:25   SECTION C-C, SCALE 1:25

TOP LEFT
Modest variations in wall colours match the patinations of the antique work bench and wall-mounted drawers and contrast with the flat painted MDF elements on the opposite wall.

TOP RIGHT
The colour of the new façade continues in the interior in the painted MDF shelving that runs the length of one existing wall.

MIDDLE LEFT
When opened to the room the colours of the kitchen sit comfortably with those of the shelving wall.

MIDDLE RIGHT
An oak base supports the top of local stone on the meeting place table. The simplicity of the circle cut in the timber pull strip that runs the height of the sliding doors blends with the simplicity of the existing shell.

BOTTOM
Flat green/blue paint connects the dark interior to the exterior space. Corrugated metal cladding makes no attempt to blur the line between old and new.

CONTACT DETAILS

3Gatti Architecture Studio
Floor 2 Office K
169 Jinxian Road
200020 Shanghai
China
T: +86 21 62 08 79 89
E: shanghai-office@3gatti.com
www.3gatti.com
Red Object

Annvil
Anna Butele
Kalnciema Street 37
Riga, Latvia LV-1046
T: +371 29391461
E: anna@annvil.lv
www.annvil.lv
Annvil Office; Hills + Knowlton

Atelier RAW s.r.o.
Domazlicka 12
612 00 Brno
Czech Republic
T: +420 541 242 908
E: atelier@raw.cz
www.raw.cz
KKCG

Barbara Appolloni Arquitecta
Passeig de l'Exposicio 113
113 Baixos
08004 Barcelona
Spain
T: +34 645 816 268
E:info@barbaraappolloni.com
www.barbaraappolloni.com
Studio Appolloni

Brinkworth
4-6 Ellsworth Street
London E2 0AX
UK
T: +44(0)20 7613 5341
E: info@brinkworth.co.uk
www.brinkworth.co.uk
LBi; Venture 3

Corvin Cristian
3 Pictor Stahi Street
Bucharest
Romania
T: +40 744 537 079
E: corvin@corvincristian.com
www.corvin@corvincristian.com
Headvertising

EHA (Ector Hoogstad Architects)
Laanslootseweg 1
3028 HT Rotterdam
PO Box 818
3000 AV Rotterdam
The Netherlands
T: +31 10 440 21 21
E: info@ectorhoogstad.com
www.ectorhoogstad.com
IMd

Elding Oscarson
Hammarby Fabriksvag 43
Plan 6 120 30
Stockholm
Sweden
E: info@eldingoscarson.com
www.eldingoscarson.com
No Picnic

Eriksen Skajaa Arkitekter AS
St Halvards Plass 1
0192 Oslo
Norway
E: post@eriksenskajaa.no
www.eriksenskajaa.no
Bergen; Netlife

Graven Images
175 Albion Street
Glasgow G1 1RU
UK
T: +44 141 552 6626
E: info@graven.co.uk
www.graven.co.uk
**Business Stream; Glasgow Life;
Student Loan Company**

Groosman Partners Architecten
Schouwburgplein 34
3012 CL Rotterdam
The Netherlands
T: +31 10 201 40 00
E: info@gp.nl
www.gp.nl
RDM Innovation Dock

H2O Architectes
18 Rue Du Sentier
Paris 75002
France
T: +33 (0) 9 64 00 52 81
E: contact@h2oarchitectes.com
www.h2oarchitectes.com
Hypernuit

i29
Industrieweg 29
1115 AD Duivendrecht
The Netherlands
T: +31 20 695 61 20
E: info@i29.nl
www.i29.nl
Social 01; Office 04

**LOJO (Logan and Johnson
Associates)**
1507 Hawthorne Street
Houston, TX 77006
USA
T: +1 720 427 4495
E: office@logan and Johnson.com
www.loganandjohnson.com
Sierra Club

Mancini Enterprises
17 Crescent Avenue
Kesavaperumalpuram
600028 Chennai
India
T: +91 44 2461 4000
E: architects@mancini-design.com
www.mancini-design.com
TVS

Masquespacio
Roger de lauria 11, 1
46002 Valencia
Spain
T: +34 96 352 77 56
E: info@masquespacio.com
www.masquespacio.com
Zapata y Herrera

Ministry of Design
20 Cross Street
03-01 Singapore 048422
E: studio@modonline.com
www.modonline.com
Bar Code

Morpho Studio
Justyna Freidberg
Ul. Przemyslowa
12 30-701 Krakow
Poland
T: +48 506 148 268
E: justyna@morphostudio.pl
www.morphostudio.pl
Pride and Glory Interactive

MVRDV
Dunantstraat 10
3024 BC Rotterdam
The Netherlands
T: +31 (0)10 477 2860
E: office@mvrdv.com
www.mvrdv.nl
Teletech

Openbox Company Limited
264/3 New Road 80
Bangkolame, Bkk 10120
Thailand
T: +66 2688844
E: openbox@openbox.in.th
www.openbox.in.th
Vanachai

Origins Architecten
Schieweg 210
2636 KA Schipluiden
The Netherlands
T: +31 10477 81 31
E: info@origins-architecten.nl
www.origins-architecten.nl
Onesize

PS Arkitektur AB
Kvarngatan 14
118 47 Stockholm
Sweden
T: +46 (0) 8 702 06 30
E: info@psarkitektur.se
www.psarkitektur.com
Skype

Rapt Studio
111 Maiden Lane
Suite 350
San Francisco
CA 94108
USA
T: +1 415 788 4400
E: info@raptstudio.com
www.raptstudio.com
Adobe

Selgascano
Guecho 27
28023 Madrid
Spain
Tel: +34 913076481
E: selgascano3@gmail.com
www.selgascano.net
Office In The Woods

ABOUT THE CD

Sid Lee Architecture
75 Queen Street
Suite 150
Montreal (Quebec)
H3C 2N6
Canada
E: media@sidlee.com
www.sidleearchitecture.com
Red Bull

SO-IL
68 Jay Street 501
Brooklyn
New York
NY 11201
USA
T: +1 718 624-6666
E: office@so-il.org
www.so-il.org
Logan

Stephen Williams Associates
Admiralitatstrasse 71
20459 Hamburg
Germany
T: +49 (0)40 879 33 40 0
E: mail@stephenwilliams.com
www.stephenwilliams.com
Jung von Matt

Stone Designs
C/Segovia 10
28005 madrid
Spain
T: +34 91 540 03 36
E: info@stone-dsgns.com
www.stone-dsgns.com
Ymedia

Studio SKLIM
E: info@sklim.com
www.sklim.com
Thin Office

Swine Studio
20 Mendip House
Welwyn Street
London E2 OJW
UK
E: info@studioswine.com
www.studioswine.com
Emu Films

Taranta Creations
N.18, 506 West Jianguo Road
Xuhui, Shanghai 200031
China
T: +86 21 54488192
E: info@enrico-taranta.com
www.enrico-taranta.com
Red Town

Terhivatal
Pasareti ut 24
1026 Budapest
Hungary
E: ternhivatal@gmail.com
www.tervhivatal.hu
Goldberger

TT Architects
Motoya Building 4F
16-14 Kawanishi
Kurashiki
Okayama 710-0812
Japan
T: +81 (86) 441 6032
E: info@ttarchi.com
www.ttarchi.com
Kawanishi Fam

Universal Design Studio
37-42 Charlotte Road
London EC2A 3PG
UK
T: +44 (0)20 7033 3881
E: info@universaldesignstudio.com
www.universaldesignstudio.com
Mulberry

Upsetters Architects
5A 3-2-11 Nishiazabu
Minato-ku
Tokyo 106-0031
Japan
T: +81 3-5775-5775
E: info@upsetters.jp
www.upsetters.jp
WOW

Urban Salon
16 Stannary Street
London SE11 4AA
UK
T: +44 20 7735 5327
E: mail@urbansalonarchitects.com
www.urbansalonarchitects.com
BBH

Vrtiška Žák
Na Zderaze 1947/3
120 00
Praha 2
Czech Republic
E: studio@vrtiskazak.com
www.vrtiskazak.com
KKCG

The attached CD can be read on both Windows and Macintosh computers. All the material on the CD is copyright protected and is for private use only. The CD includes files for all of the drawings included in the book where available. The drawings for each building are contained in a folder labelled with the project name. They are supplied in two versions: the files with the suffix '.eps' are 'vector' Illustrator EPS files but can be opened using other graphics programs such as Photoshop; all the files with the suffix '.dwg' are generic CAD format files and can be opened in a variety of CAD programs.

Each image file is numbered according to its original location within the book and within a project, reading from left to right and top to bottom of the page, followed by the scale. Hence, '01_01_200.eps' would be the eps version of the first drawing of the first project in the book and has a scale of 1:200.

The generic '.dwg' file format does not support 'solid fill' utilized by many architectural CAD programs. All the information is embedded within the file and can be reinstated within supporting CAD programs. Select the polygon required and change the 'Attributes' to 'Solid', and the colour information should be automatically retrieved. To reinstate the 'Walls'; select all objects within the 'Walls' layer/ class and amend their 'Attributes' to 'Solid'.

CREDITS

Images are supplied courtesy of the architects and designers. In all cases every effort has been made to credit the copyright holders, but should there be any omissions or errors the publisher will be pleased to insert the appropriate acknowledgment in any subsequent editions of the book.

Adobe
Rapt Studio
Photography: Eric Laignel and Weston Colton

Annvil Office
Designer: Anna Butele, Annvil
Photography: Ingus Bajars

Bar Code
Ministry of Design: Colin Seah
Contractor: Interior Composite
Photography: CI&A Photography, Edward Hendricks

BBH
Urban Salon
Photography: Gareth Gardner

Bergen
Eriksen Skajaa Arkitekter AS
Photography: Arkitekturfotograf Rasmus Norlander

Business Stream
Graven Images
Photography: Renzo Mazzolini

Emu Office
Swine Studio: Alexander Groves and Azusa Murakami
Photographs courtesy Swine Studio

Glasgow Life, Glasgow City Council
Graven Images
Photography: Renzo Mazzolini

Goldberger
Terhivatal: Zsanett Benedek & Daniel Lakos
Box interiors: Wanda Reich and Noemi Varga
Photography: Tamas Bujnovszky

Headvertising
Corvin Cristian
Photography: Vlad Caprarescu
(vlad@smartfilm.ro)

Hills Knowlton
Annvil: Anna Butele
Photography: Aleksejs Belokopitovs

Hypernuit
H2O Architectes
Charlotte Hibert/Jean-Jacque Hubert/Antoine Santiard; Photography: Julien Attard (www.julienattard.com)

Jung von Matt
Stephen Williams Associates
Project team: Stephen Williams, Julia Erdmann, Daniel Konig, Lucia Kons

Kawanishi Fam
TT Architects: Teruki Takayoshi
Contractor: Meguro Construction
Photography: Kei Sugino

KKCG
Vrtiška • Žák/ Atelier RAW
Photography: Kristina. Hrabetova

Lbi
Brinkworth
Photography: Alex Franklin

IMd
EHA Architects
Project team: Joost Ector, Max Pape, Chris Arts, Markus Clarijs, Hetty Mommersteeg, Arja Hoogstad, Paul Sanders, Roel Widervamck, Ridwan Tehupelasury
Installation Design: Unica
Structural advice: iMd Consulting Engineers
Building physics: LBP Sight
Fixed furnishing: L.P. van Vliet – interior architects
Furniture design: Ector Hoogstad Architects
Contractor: De Combi
Photography: Petra Appelhof

Logan
SO-IL
Project team: Florian Idenburg, Jing Liu, Ilias Papageorgiou (associate principal in charge)
General contractor: Katsura Construction
Work surface fabrication: Situ Studio
Lighting consultation: Lighting workshop
Felt: Felt Studio
Photography: Iwan Baan, Naho Kubota

Mulberry
Universal Design Studio
Photography: Paul Greenleaf

Netlife
Eriksen Skajaa Arkitekter AS
Photography: Ivan Brodey

No Picnic
Elding Oscarson
Photography: Ake E:son Lindman

Office In The Woods
Selgascano: Lucia Cano and Jose Selgas in collaboration with Jose de Villar.
Metal structure: TCI Industrial Technical Metalwork; Polyester walls: Ursa Fiberline; Walls, internal partitions and shelves: Methacrylate Industries; Wood paving and furniture: Bascope Carpenters; Electricity and communications: Elsues; Plumbing: Martin Juez
Photography: Iwan Baan and Roland Halbe

Onesize
Origins Architecten
Architect: Jaime van Lede
Photography: Stijnstijl (www.stijnstijl)

Pride and Glory Interactive
Morpho Studio: Justyna Freidberg
Photography: Hanna Długosz

RDM Innovation Dock
Architecture: Groosman Partners Architecten
Interior design: Groosman Partners Interieur
Project architect: Gert de Graaf
Project team: Jan-Erik Broere, Jorien Zwartsenburg
Contractor: Era Contour, Zoetermeer

Consultants building physics and installations: DWA, Bodegraven
Structural engineer: Pieters Bouwtechniek B.V., Delft
Photography: Theo Peekstok (Groosman Partners)

Red Bull
Architectural design: Sid Lee Architecture Montreal
Visual identity and graphic design: Sid Lee Amsterdam
Local architects: Kamstra Architecten BNA
Builders: Fiction Factory
Furniture: 2D&W
General contractors: Jora Vision B.V.
Photography: Ewout Huibers

Red Object
3Gatti Architecture Studio
Designer: Francesco Gatti
Project manager: Ingrid Pu
Collaborators: Paolo Riceci, candy Zhang, Vivian Husiyue, Ben Hou, Peter Ye, Sunny Wang, Chen han Yi, Robin Feng
Engineer: Jachy Yan
Contractor: K2Lab
Photgrahy: Masato Kawano (Nacasa & Partners Inc)

Red Town
Taranta Creations
Design team: Enrico Taranta, Juriaan Calis, Giorgio Radoikovic
Photography: Shen Qiang of Shen Photo

Sierra Club
LOJO (Logan and Johnson Associates)
Project team: Matthew Johnson, Jason Logan
Photography: Matthew Johnson

Skype
PS Arkitektur AB
Principal architect: Peter Sahlin
Stage 1–Project architect: Mette Larsson Wedborn; Assistants: Erika Janunger and Therese Svalling
Stage 2–Project architect: Mari Owrenn; Assistants: Martina Eliasson, Emilie Westergaard Folkersen, Therese Svalling
Lighting design: Beata Denton
Photography: Jason Strong Photography

Social 01
i29
Photography: i29

Student Loans Company
Graven Images
Photography: Renzo Mazzolini

Studio Appolloni
Barbara Appolloni Arquitecta
Photographs courtesy Barbara Appoloni

Teletech
MVRDV: Winy Maas, Jacob van Rijs and Natalie de Vries
with Fokke Moerel, Bertrand Schippan, Catherine Drieux, Rune Veile, Macieje Zawadzki and David Sebastian
Co-architects: Arkos Concepteurs Associes; Seturec Architecture

Consultants–Structure: ET.BAT; Services: AGICCES; Quality control: DEKRA; Acoustics: Acoustique France; Geotechnical: Geotec; Security: Prosseco
Contractor: Curot, longvic, Cedex
Photography: Jeroen Musch

Thin Office
Studio SKLIM
Photography: Jeremy San

Office 04
i29
Contractor: Grontmij
Furniture manufacture: Zwartwoud (custom-made pieces)
Photography: i29

TVS
Mancini Enterprises
Project team: Niels Schoenfelder, J.T. Arima, R. Saravanan, A Sridharan, Rijesh K., Divya Khullar Narayanan, Shilpa Ramadurga, Hari D.S., Nameer Nasir, Meera Murali, Syed Arshad, Safia Fidha, Srinath Syresh
Executing architect: Bhaskar Architect
MEP consultants: Suranam Engineering Services Pvt. Ltd.
Photography: Mohandass Radhakrishnan + Pavendran Jayaprakash

Vanachai
Openbox Company Limited
Lighting: FOS Lighting Studio
Structure: Openbox Company Limited
Mechanical and Electrical: MITR Consultant
Photography: Wison Tungthunya
Landscape: Openbox Compamy Limited

Venture 3
Brinkworth
Photographs courtesy of Brinkworth

WOW
Upsetters Architects
Photography: Yusuke Wakabayashi

Ymedia
Stone Designs: Eva Prego and Cutu Mazuelos
Photographs courtesy of Stone Designs

Zapata y Herrera
Masquespacio
Design: Ana Milena Hernandez Palacios
Contractor: Jose Manual Paz Agra Construcciones
Photography: David Rodriquez of Cualiti